THE FUTURE COMES

THE FUTURE COMES

A Study of the New Deal

By
CHARLES A. BEARD
and
GEORGE H. E. SMITH

GREENWOOD PRESS, PUBLISHERS
WESTPORT, CONNECTICUT

330.973
6 3 o 8 f

The Library of Congress has catalogued this publication as follows:

Library of Congress Cataloging in Publication Data

Beard, Charles Austin, 1874-1948.
  The future comes.

    1. United States—Economic policy—1933-1945.
2. Industry and state—United States. 3. National
Industrial Recovery Act, 1933. 4. United States—
Politics and government—1933-1945. I. Smith,
George Howard Edward, 1898-1962, joint author.
II. Title.
HC106.3.B42 1972   330.9'73'0917   73-143307
ISBN 0-8371-5808-7

HC
106·3
.B42
1972

Originally published in 1933
by The Macmillan Company, New York

Reprinted with the permission
of William Beard, Mrs. Miriam Vagts and
Mrs. Josephine B. Smith

First Greenwood Reprinting 1972

Library of Congress Catalogue Card Number 73-143307

ISBN 0-8371-5808-7

Printed in the United States of America

PREFACE

This volume is a by-product of a larger work, on national interest, which Mr. Smith and I are writing. The first volume of that work, entitled *The Idea of National Interest,* now in press, is historical, analytical, and descriptive in character. The second volume, in preparation, represents an effort to construct a convenient philosophy of national interest. Although the larger work deals mainly with the international aspects of the subject, it recognizes the often neglected fact that domestic and foreign affairs are parts of the same thing and cannot be separated in fact, whatever formalists may do for their particular purposes. In the preparation of that work, therefore, it became necessary to consider certain questions bearing on internal economy. Can national interest in foreign relations be anything other than a reflection of public interest in the domestic field? What is the prevailing conception of public interest in the contemporary political thought and action of the United States?

An examination of these questions led inevitably to an inquiry into the trends of American economy and public policy. That inquiry involved a careful survey of the measures and policies of the administration of President Franklin D. Roosevelt, with a view to preparing a summary and interpretation for our volume on the philosophy of national interest.

In connection with the larger enterprise, I sketched the outline of the survey and the proposed chapter and assembled a large mass of materials bearing on the project. These I turned over to my colleague, Mr. Smith, and he then drafted a tentative report. His report seemed to me to be a genuine contribution to an understanding of the startling events which have occurred since March 4, 1933. It contained a large body of concrete information, collected from numerous sources not readily available to students of current politics. It presented the main issues in an orderly fashion. It was done in a scholarly temper.

It therefore occurred to me that citizens interested in clues to the swift and bewildering movement of contemporary affairs might find in these pages some convenient information and helpful guidance. So I went over Mr. Smith's report with great care, making revisions and modifications here and there, and prepared for publication the whole document originally intended to be an aid for the memory in the construction of our larger work on national interest.

This volume, then, is a joint product, in the sense that I drafted the first project, furnished a large body of materials, and revised the whole. But it is only fair to say that Mr. Smith has borne the lion's share of the burden.

CHARLES A. BEARD.

New Milford, Conn.,
Nov. 10. 1933.

INTRODUCTION

Owing to the nature of the circumstances surrounding the preparation of this volume, as indicated in the Preface, interest centers in events between March 4, 1933, and November 1, 1933. For that reason the text makes an arbitrary break in history. Whether March 4, 1933, will mark the beginning of an epoch only the history of the future can determine. Behind the events that have occurred since that day lies a long chain of events. Those who live and think in terms of daily headlines are likely to forget that the New Deal grows inexorably out of the Old Deal; that it is a phase of larger history which embraces all times and occurrences.

Accordingly, observers who are inclined to imagine that President Roosevelt is making history and to forget that he is also a victim of history will get a false perspective from the following pages standing alone. It is necessary to be on guard against the delusion of the absolutely "new" epoch. What appears to be new is often really a matter of emphasis rather than of creation *de novo*.

The question of the public policy to be applied to the immense concentration in American industry—to the steady collectivization of American economy—has long been before the country. One school of statesmen has

consistently insisted on "breaking up the trusts" and
has sponsored legislation to that end, undiscouraged by
the patent failure of their efforts. On the other hand,
another school of statesmen has taken the view that
this movement in concentration would inevitably require an adjustment of political policy and action in
keeping with the collectivism of the facts.

Woodrow Wilson's *New Freedom* was based on the
old tradition and the answer of history since 1914 has
been a demonstration of its inapplicability and futility.
Although a member of the same Jeffersonian party,
President Franklin D. Roosevelt repudiates the New
Freedom in economy, accepts the inexorable collectivism of American economy in fact, and seeks to work
out a policy based on recognition of the main course
of our economic history. President Coolidge and President Hoover accepted the main course of our economic
history, but proposed to make no fundamental readjustment in public policy as a result of that acceptance.
Therein seems to lie the event that differentiates the
thought of President Franklin D. Roosevelt from that
of his immediate predecessors and gives a semblance
of reality to the use of the term "new" in connection
with his "deal."

In making note of continuity in history, we are also
compelled to regard all that has happened since March
4, 1933, as a phase of a movement which will occupy
the coming years and centuries. The opposition to
President Roosevelt's policies and measures, already
taking form on a large scale, will likewise have to
reckon with the old question: What is to be done about

the inexorable concentration which accompanies large-scale industry? Here the ancient issues appear, like demons from the pit: What can be done, if anything? What is desirable? Who is to decide on desirability? Can those who decide on a project of desirability give effect to their desire? How can they do it—by the democratic or the dictatorial process?

Within this frame of reference, momentous decisions will be made in the coming months—by President Roosevelt himself, and by those who would make different history themselves. These decisions will be interesting to the student of world history as distinguished from the statesman intent on the instant need of things; and they may well be fateful, beyond all measurement.

It is presumptuous, of course, to attempt a scientific classification of the various aspects included in the Recovery Program, except in the broadest terms. No nation can live through a war, fought on such a scale as was the World War, without sustaining scars deeper even than the slaughter of its manhood on the field of battle. No nation can lead in the creation of a new technological revolution without seeing the old economic foundations shattered almost beyond repair. No nation can raise up out of the ruins of a tottering monarchical system a Great Democracy, and try to make of it a living, breathing, reality in the lives of its whole people, without feeling reverberations throughout the roots and branches of society.

The United States did all three. It entered and fought in the war with unremitting zeal. It brought mass production to the highest stage of perfection and began the third transformation of industry—into the age of electric power. It has built up a Great Democracy, and by wide opportunity, broad tolerance, and universal education, sought to make of democracy an enduring principle in social life. It could not do these things —even one of them—without raising serious, challenging, almost insuperable problems. They are not problems of the past; nor are they "academic." They are immediate problems, and their solution lies in the future.

Whoever traces far any one of the major problems facing the Roosevelt administration on March 4, 1933 —the veterans' benefits, the war debts and post-war finance, the stagnation of industry, the weakened railroads, the prostrate farms, the colossal public and private debt, the concentration of wealth—will find its roots deeply imbedded in one or more of the three world developments in which the United States played a vital part. Moreover, each single problem is itself complex, and ranges into the fields of other problems which, on the surface at least, seem not to have the remotest connection. The National Industrial Recovery Act, for example, has its political and social, as well as its purely economic, aspects. The Emergency Banking Act, the Glass-Steagall Banking Act, the Agricultural Adjustment Act, are each of them inextricably woven into the very fabric of the whole society.

Any classification of the Recovery Program must therefore be a broad and arbitrary one. It must admit the possibility of other arrangements of the materials—

the acts and developments—since March 4. It must admit that many inter-relationships may be obscured. Chronological presentations will be found to be ignored wherever clarity and understanding may be better served in some other way. Extreme detail could scarcely be expected in a document of this limited size. At some points, details will be fully considered and especially emphasized; at others, only summarily treated; all according as the conception of the whole document may dictate. Unconscious error is freely admitted as probable, but deliberate distortion has been anxiously avoided. Such convictions as may be expressed—and there will be many of them—rest on a study of relevant facts.

The Recovery Program itself seems to fall logically into five broad fields: Government, Industry and Transportation, Agriculture, Finance, and Relief. In the field of Government, the major operations concern the budget, the political structure, and administration. Questions bearing upon the monetary system should have a place there too, but for convenience of treatment they are discussed under Finance. In Industry and Transportation, the National Industrial Recovery Act and the Emergency Railroad Transportation Act are the chief considerations. The Agricultural Adjustment Act is the outstanding factor in the field of Agriculture. The banking acts, the Securities Act, credit, inflation and the gold situation, fall in the field of Finance. A broad conception is held of the field of Relief. Not only does it embrace essential distress relief, but it also covers national employment agencies, the Civilian Conservation Corps, public works, relief to mortgage debtors—urban and rural—and other acts and devices of a remedial character which are more specific and direct than broadly general in scope.

In developing each subject the legislative situation will be set forth first wherever possible. It will be followed by a treatment of the organization and administrative machinery set up to carry out the legislation. And finally, the operations will be briefly considered in the light of current information. The consideration will be mainly expository, except for observations here and there. Some of the principles back of the Recovery Program will appear from the factual presentation of the Program, but, in the main, these principles and some appraisal of them will form the subject of a separate part of this document.

CONTENTS

THE FUTURE COMES

CHAPTER I

A BACKGROUND FOR THE CRISIS OF
MARCH 4, 1933

"THIS is pre-eminently the time to speak the truth, the whole truth, frankly and boldly . . . the only thing we have to fear is fear itself—nameless, unreasoning, unjustified terror. . . ." The President was speaking. It was his inaugural address. His voice, carried by radio throughout the land, fell upon the ears of a people profoundly stirred by the impact of recent events.

It was in the early morning hours of February 14 that the Governor of Michigan issued a proclamation temporarily closing all financial institutions throughout the state. The order came without warning. True, the general public had been apprehensive over the depressed condition of the country, but the people were not prepared for such a dramatic turn of events. To the nation at large, the Michigan crisis gave a concrete and terrifying meaning to the widespread uneasiness, just as would a cry of "Fire" in a crowded theater where the smell of smoke was already heavy in the air. Bewilderment gave way to blind fear when in the ensuing few days an increasing number of other states restricted withdrawals of banking funds. On February 24, a three-day state-wide banking holiday was proclaimed by the Governor of Maryland. A rush to convert bank deposits into cash swept the country. The drain of cash from the money centers grew to enormous proportions, raising the level of money in circulation to a reported high record of approximately seven and a half billions of dollars. In the confusion born of fear, cash was the symbol of safety just as is the lifeboat of an ocean liner at the moment of sudden distress at sea, although in either case a stampede may make safety for all impossible.

By March 4 the banks in every state were either closed or operating under severe restrictions. In Washington the President was recording the grim realities that were even then seething beneath the colorful display of a national ceremony. "Only a foolish optimist can deny the dark realities of the moment," he said. "Practices of the unscrupulous money changers stand indicted in the court of public opinion," he declared. "Yes, the money changers have fled from their high seats in the temple of our civilization." And what a severe indictment it had been! In the few days preceding the inaugural ceremonies at Washington, the "money changers" had been *driven* from their high places by a frantic popular demand for cash that had assumed the nature of a national panic.

"We may now restore that temple to the ancient truths," the President continued. Restoration calls for more than changes in ethics alone. "This nation asks for action, and action now." Indeed the financial crisis confronting the nation could admit of no cavil. It required a swift and decisive move to break the panic and end the drain on the nation's stocks of money. Before the dawn of another business day, acting under the unrepealed war powers granted to Woodrow Wilson in the Act of October 6, 1917, President Roosevelt issued a proclamation closing the banks throughout the nation.

His act was the culmination of more than three years of increasingly intense economic distress. The banking holiday marked the almost complete prostration of the nation at a time when, fundamentally, it had attained its greatest material strength. "Our distress comes from no failure of substance," the President had declared. "Plenty is at our doorstep, but a generous use of it languishes in the very sight of the supply." Yet three years of crashing prices, unsalable commodity surpluses, restricted credits, failing banks, closed factories, increasing unemployment, and the breakdown of distress relief, had weakened the nation, undermined the morale of its people, and had driven them into an unreasoned raid upon the money stocks of the country in a desperate but vain attempt to insure self-preservation.

The causes of the collapse are still the subject of debate, but the evidences of the débâcle were all too painfully obvious. They could be seen beneath the surface of "prosperity" in the late spring and summer of 1929, but they did not break through until the morning of October 29, 1929.

The big gong had hardly sounded in the great hall of the Exchange at ten o'clock Tuesday morning before the storm broke in full force. Huge blocks of stock were thrown

upon the market for what they would bring. . . . Not only
were small traders being sold out, but big ones, too. . . .
Again and again the specialist in a stock would find himself
surrounded by brokers fighting to sell—and nobody at all
even thinking of buying. . . . The scene on the floor was
chaotic. . . . Within half an hour of the opening the volume of trading passed three million shares, by twelve
o'clock it had passed eight million, by half-past one it had
passed twelve million, and when the closing gong brought
the day's madness to an end the gigantic record of 16,410,-
030 shares had been set . . . the average prices of fifty
leading stocks, as compiled by the New York *Times*, had
fallen nearly forty points.*

Sales on the New York Stock Exchange for the
month of October, 1929, as reported by the *Annalist*,
reached the enormous volume of 141,668,000 shares.
The ensuing deflation during the subsequent three
years is less picturesquely recorded in the cold statistics of major business conditions. A few of these will
suffice to indicate the blows which battered the country and wore down the morale of its people.

Unless otherwise stated the period covered in the
following computations is from September, 1929, to
January, 1933. According to the Dow-Jones index of
stock prices, 30 industrials fell from an average of
364.9 to 62.7 dollars per share. A group of 20 public
utilities stocks dropped from 141.9 to 28.0 dollars per
share. Twenty railroad stocks declined from an average
of 182.0 to 28.1 dollars per share. Other indexes recorded the same catastrophe. According to the New
York *Times* index of 50 stocks (25 industrials and 25

* Frederick L. Allen, *Only Yesterday.*

railroads) the average price fell from 300.52 to 58.65 dollars per share. A compilation by the Standard Statistics Co. (Inc.) of 421 stocks (351 industrials, 37 public utilities, and 33 railroads) based upon an index number of 100 as the 1926 monthly average, showed a decline from 225.2 to 49.1 from September, 1929, to January, 1933. According to the same source and during the same period, the index of 20 New York bank stocks fell from 357.8 to 67.9.

The net profits of corporations, as compiled by the Federal Reserve Bank of New York from the quarterly reports of 500 diversified companies, declined from 939 millions of dollars in September, 1929, to 183.3 millions in September, 1932, with countless firms reporting actual deficits. Only cash dividend and interest payments seemed to offer a stubborn and sustained resistance to the tremendous pressure of the deflation. The monthly average of dividend payments, as compiled (from the reports of a limited number of companies) by the New York *Journal of Commerce,* was (in thousands of dollars) as follows: for 1929, 289,858; 1930, 352,138; 1931, 306,092; and for 1932, 203,241. Even allowing for changes and qualifications in the compilation, the course of dividend payments is clear. The monthly average of interest payments, recorded at the same source, shows a similar situation. In 1929 they showed a total (in thousands of dollars) of 342,-496 as the monthly average; in 1930 they rose to 364,534; in 1931 to 379,427; in 1932 to 380,389. In June, 1929, Moody's Investors Service began a survey of the cash dividend payments at current rates of 600 companies which includes practically every stock traded in on the exchange. From this compilation the monthly average of cash dividend payments at current rates for the six months period, July to December, 1929, was 2,549.6 millions of dollars; the monthly average over the full year of 1930 was 2,601.9 millions of dollars; in 1931, the monthly average dropped to 2,134.7; and in 1932, it stood at 1,326.9 millions of dollars, indicating that it was not until recent months that dividends began to recede substantially in the face of widespread deflation in all other aspects.*

The composite index of industrial production prepared by the Standard Statistics Corporation (based upon the year 1926 as 100) fell from 110 in 1929 to 48 in 1932. The physical volume of trade, according to the clearing index of business of the Federal Reserve Bank of New York (with the year 1926 as 100),

---

* Because of the incompleteness of the statistics and the technical qualifications necessarily associated with dividend and interest payments, the figures given in the text above are used merely to indicate the trend. The New York *Journal of Commerce* dividend statistics are based on returns from only such companies reporting to it, the *Wall Street Journal,* and other publications; and do not cover the same companies each month. The *Moody's Investor's Service* index is based upon stocks identical for the entire period covered. When the survey was begun, 80 per cent of the total number of stocks was on a cash dividend basis, although this percentage has subsequently been reduced. The method of computation is as follows: For each of the 600 companies a monthly record is made of the total annual cash dividends which would be paid on the basis of the most recently announced rate. Each month's aggregate of dividends for all 600 companies is then divided by the total number of shares outstanding during the month, after adjusting for stock dividends and splits in order to eliminate the effects of changes in share capitalization, to obtain the average dividend rate per share. For a more complete statement on dividend and interest payments see *Survey of Current Business* (U. S. Dept. of Commerce) Annual Supplement, 1932, and current monthly numbers of the same periodical.

dropped from 103 in 1929 to 62 in 1932; and to 54 in January, 1933.

Conclusive figures on unemployment were never available. They are not even available to-day, which is a sad commentary on our fact-finding agencies and a major indictment against the scientific exactitude of our modern economic organization. But however inexact certain estimates may be they are sufficient to indicate the state of affairs. There is enough agreement among a number of estimators to establish the fact that even during the years of "prosperity" prior to 1929, the unemployed numbered approximately two million persons annually. Estimates given by Mr. William Green, president of the American Federation of Labor, at the hearings on the bill proposing a thirty-hour work week, indicate the course of unemployment under the impact of deflation. In April, 1930, there were 2,954,000 persons out of work; by October, 1930, the number had increased to 3,924,000; by October, 1931, the total unemployed had risen to 6,801,000; and by October, 1932, the total stood at 10,908,000. During the first two months of 1933, the number rose to 12,000,000, and less reliable estimates placed the total even higher. The Federal Reserve Board's unadjusted combined index of factory employment (with the monthly average of 1923-1925 as 100) fell from 105.4 in September, 1929, to 58.1 in January, 1933; and this was regarded as conservative.

The farmer bore the full brunt of the war's aftermath in domestic life. He did not participate in the "prosperity" of the "new era" in the years before 1929.

Writing in the September 25, 1932, issue of the New York *Times,* Bernhard Ostrolenk traced the plight of the farmer during the post-war decade. The value of farm property fell off by twenty billions of dollars. More than 450,000 full owners lost their farms; and farm tenancies increased by more than 200,000. Gross annual farm income dropped from approximately sixteen billions of dollars to eleven billions. But this was not all. The farmer was yet to feel the full effects of the years since 1929. Between 1929 and 1932, farm values suffered a further decline of 33 per cent. His gross income, already sharply reduced by 1929, declined by 57 per cent to $5,143,000,000 in 1932, the Department of Agriculture announced. In 1930, the farmer was faced with a mortgage debt of 9,241 millions of dollars as against only 3,320 millions in 1910. Much of his debt had been incurred in the years after 1915 in a magnificent response to win the war. He never recovered from his precarious position. It was impossible to break free from his bondage to finance, unless he bowed down to the ruthless deflationary device of foreclosure. Foreclosure would destroy his independence, wrench him from his home and the soil, and either make of him a tenant farmer or cast him adrift in a world already hopelessly overcrowded with men and women seeking a chance to earn a living. All the while, general economic conditions operated to beat down the prices for the commodities the farmer produced and to keep up the prices of the goods he had to buy. On the basis of the average level of prices for the period 1910-1914 as 100, the prices received by the farmer stood at the index number of 205 in 1920; 147 in 1925; 139 in 1928; 117 in 1930; and 51 in January, 1933. On the other hand, the downward trend of the prices of the goods the farmer had to buy was not nearly so drastic. Based on the same index, the prices paid by the farmers dropped from 206 in 1920 to only 105 in 1932.

Other economic conditions operated to intensify the swirl of the downward spiral between 1929 and January, 1933. The load of debt borne by the people was an oppressive burden. In a statement placed before the Senate Finance Committee investigating economic conditions, Irving Fisher of Yale University estimated the total debts owing in the United States in 1929 at 234 billions of dollars as compared with 362 billions as the total wealth of the United States. According to a compilation of the National Industrial Conference Board, the total interest-bearing debt was estimated at 154,761 millions of dollars in 1929. It embraced a farm indebtedness of approximately twelve and a quarter billions, a steam railroad debt of twelve and three-quarter billions, a total public debt of over thirty billions, a corporate debt of close to seventy-five billions, and individual indebtedness (other than farmers) of twenty-five billions. After three years of deflation and liquidation, the debt still totaled 134 billions of dollars according to a study of the Twentieth Century Fund released in the spring of 1933. During the same period the national income had fallen from eighty-five to forty billions of dollars.

Some 37 cities reported the existence of deplorable

conditions and recorded the breakdown of relief in the spring of 1932. A few months later, a survey of 126 cities, representing 56 per cent of the urban population of the United States, reported relief aid to 823,894 families in May, 1932, as against 386,151 families of the year before. Relief expenditures of New York City set at approximately one million dollars in October, 1929, rose to nine and a half millions in February, 1933. The Committee on the Costs of Medical Care reported "appalling" conditions in the South where the incomes of the people in ten southern states were so low that they were unable to purchase adequate medical care. School budgets were drastically cut, salaries of teachers were reduced and then deferred in many localities, teachers were dismissed and classes doubled, the term was shortened.

The American people for a time bore all these blows with remarkable fortitude, but a definite change in temper appeared in the spring of 1932. In May the railway brotherhoods presented a plea to President Hoover. It had an ominous note in it. "Mr. President," it stated, "we have come here to tell you that unless something is done to provide employment and relieve distress among the families of the unemployed, we cannot be responsible for the orderly operations of the railroads of this country—that we will refuse to take the responsibility for the disorder which is sure to arise if conditions continue. . . . The unemployed citizens whom we represent will not accept starvation while the two major political parties struggle for control of government. . . . We are not Socialists, we are

not Communists, nor are we anarchists. . . . There is
a growing demand that the entire business and social
structure be changed because of the general dissatisfaction with the present system. We cannot longer ignore
this situation."

Starting in the West and spreading rapidly throughout the country, whole communities were turning to
barter in the effort to provide relief and to break the
business stagnation. Their effort was to force the flow
of the exchange of goods and services. More than 144
organizations in scores of communities over 29 states
were reported by Stuart Chase to be turning to barter,
to "wooden money," to self-liquidating printed scrip.
As 1932 drew to a close, farmers were reported "on
the march" to prevent foreclosure sales, to stop the
production and sales of products until a fair price was
assured, to end tax sales, to cut down the principal of
farm mortgages and reduce the interest rates. The law
was either reluctant or unable to cope with them, and
violence broke out here and there. In the East, labor
was growing equally restless. In a statement published
in the January issue of the magazine, *Nation's Business,* Mr. William Green, president of the American
Federation of Labor, declared: "The American trade-
union movement has been patient. . . . We gave government every opportunity to produce a remedy. We
gave management every opportunity to produce a remedy. We gave finance every opportunity. . . . We
agreed to refrain from drastic action if employers
would refrain from drastic action. . . . Finally, after
three years of suffering we, the organized workers, de-

clare to the world, enough; we shall use our might to
compel the plain remedies withheld by those whose
misfeasance caused our woe."

Under such circumstances as these, the nation was
neither in the condition nor in the mood to withstand
further blows against its resources or the morale of its
people. But the shocks continued. For more than two
years of the depression the people's faith in the essential soundness of the nation's banks had appeared to
remain unshaken. It was popularly believed that the
banks were "bursting" with money awaiting "profitable
employment." Whatever foundation existed for the
belief (providing no "run" developed) it was sustained
by broad (in some cases even well-meant) propaganda
in many fields—in finance itself, in government, among
business leaders. But confidence is an evanescent phe-
nomenon. When the feeling of security is at its strongest it may vanish in less than the twinkling of an eye.
This was soon to be demonstrated in a terrible way for
the nation.

The status of the nation's banks as of the close of the
fiscal year, June 30, 1932, compared to previous years,
was reported in the newspapers in January, 1933—the
delay in this respect was significant.* The report, com-

* A statement of the condition of the nation's banks, issued by the
Comptroller of the Currency, had been published in the New York
Times, on December 18, 1932. But it was a resources-liabilities
statement as of June 30, 1932, and it did not on its face disclose
what had happened to the banks during the fiscal year as compared
with the previous, or other, years. Moreover on the same page,
directly under the statement, an explanatory article did nothing more
than bear out the tenor of the following captions: "The Banks'
Situation: Huge Credit Reserves. The Deposits in the Country's
19,000 Banks Now Total More Than 45 Billions of Dollars."

piled by the Comptroller of the Currency, showed that from the fiscal year 1928 to the close of the fiscal year in June, 1931, bank resources and deposits had not been severely assailed. Business might be paralyzed, unemployment totals might mount alarmingly, suffering could be widespread, but the banks appeared to maintain their strength. In round numbers resources were 71½ billions in 1928; 72 billions in 1929; 74 billions in 1930; and over 70 billions in 1931. But from the latter date to the close of the fiscal year on June 30, 1932, resources dropped to $57,245,131,000. Bank deposits followed the same trend. In 1928, they totaled 58½ billions; in 1929 they stood at approximately 58 billions; in 1930 they rose to close on 60 billions; and in 1931, they were almost 57 billions. But in the next year to June 30, 1932, they fell to $45,390,269,000. A drop of close to 13 billions of dollars in resources, and almost 11½ billions in deposits, in one year was an astounding revelation; and it came at a most unfortunate time. The report also showed that in the three years ended on June 30, 1932, the number of all reporting banks declined by 6,167.

Less than three weeks later another blow came in the field of finance. The Reconstruction Finance Corporation released its quarterly statement on February 3, 1933. It contained a detailed summary of aggregate loans from the beginning of its operations on February 2, 1932, to December 31, 1932. It showed the banks and trust companies to be the largest borrowers. The number of banks and trust companies for which loans were authorized totaled 5,582; and the loans actually made over the period amounted to $850,082,060.02. This was three times the total amount of the next largest borrowers, the railroads. Such information was almost unbelievable, especially when coupled with the report of the Comptroller of the Currency in the form published in the newspapers just a few weeks before. It was not long before it began to dawn upon the people that the banks might be in serious straits; that they might not be "bursting" with money.

Whatever doubts may have existed in this perplexing situation, they were completely resolved by the declaration of the Michigan bank holiday on February 14. Money "in circulation" began to rise rapidly. In the ten days before March 4, close to $1,550,000,000 was withdrawn from the Federal Reserve system. The net loss of gold through earmarkings and other operations approximated 169.4 millions of dollars in February and 113.3 millions in March before the outflow was stopped by Executive Orders and emergency legislation. In retrospect, the April issue of the *Survey of Current Business* declared that the period from the middle of February to the middle of March was "featured by one of the most serious banking crises through which the nation has passed."

Speaking to a prostrate people, President Roosevelt drew the curtain on almost four years of confusion and economic distress. "This is because the rulers of the exchange of mankind's goods have failed through their own stubbornness and their own incompetence, have admitted their failure and have abdicated," he declared. They have tried, he granted, "but their efforts have been cast in the pattern of an outworn tradition. Faced by the failure of credit, they have proposed only the lending of more money. Stripped of the lure of profit by which to induce our people to follow their false leadership, they have resorted to exhortations, pleading tearfully for restored confidence. They know only the rules of a generation of self-seekers. They have no vision, and when there is no vision the people perish."

If we are to go forward, "we must move as a trained and loyal army willing to sacrifice for the good of a common discipline"; and we are "ready and willing to submit our lives and our property to such a discipline because it makes possible a leadership which aims at the larger good. This I propose to offer, pledging that the larger purposes will bind upon us, bind upon us all as a sacred obligation with a unity of duty hitherto evoked only in time of armed strife. With this pledge taken, I assume unhesitatingly the leadership of this great army of our people, dedicated to a disciplined attack upon our common problems."

Such was the crisis facing the nation on March 4. And such was the spirit in which a new President and a new administration entered upon "The New Deal."

CHAPTER II

THE FIRST DAYS OF THE CRISIS

IT was obvious that the crisis which the country was facing on March 4 was composed of two parts. It may be said that there were two major crises. There was the immediate emergency created by the financial breakdown. There was also the business stagnation, the enormous volume of unemployment, the failure of distress relief, and the widespread social unrest. Each one was serious. Together, they presented a formidable challenge to the new administration.

The money crisis—that is, the immediate need for banking facilities and the provision of adequate currency—was a special problem. It need not be treated as a major part of the Recovery Program. It bore the same relationship to the condition of the country as, in the case of a severed artery, the tourniquet bears to the subsequent healing process and the fundamental physical condition of the injured person. That is, although vitally necessary and indispensable, it was nevertheless an emergency affair, a special problem, and could be expected to give way before the re-emergence of the greater, the fundamental, long-term problems. It is so treated here, by way of clearing the ground for a detailed consideration of the Recovery

16

Program proper. It should be noted, however, that there were some elements involved in the immediate money crisis which eventually passed over into the Recovery Program. The problem of what to do about a large number of banks whose capital structure was seriously impaired was such an element. Those elements of the crisis which showed the need for long-term treatment and on that account passed over into the Recovery Program will be noted for later discussion under the appropriate heading.

MEETING THE IMMEDIATE FINANCIAL CRISIS

The tension throughout the country during the last week in February has already been described. State banking authorities were issuing orders aimed to conserve resources in the banks subject to their jurisdictions. The first attempt to move nationally was taken by the 72d Congress. By a joint resolution of the Senate and the House, the Comptroller of the Currency was empowered to exercise any powers with respect to national banking associations that were possessed by State officials with respect to State financial institutions.* This resolution was approved and became operative February 25, 1933. It was followed on March 3, by another resolution giving the Comptroller powers which were practically plenary " . . . to prescribe such rules and regulations as he deems advisable gov-

---

* To hold the number of references to a minimum, specific citations will be avoided where possible. Most of the material relating to the money crisis may be found in *Documents and Statements Pertaining to the Banking Emergency*, Parts I and II; United States Treasury Publications; Washington, D. C. 1933.

erning the receipt and withdrawal of deposits by and
from any such bank and trust company . . ." in the
District of Columbia. The purpose of both resolutions
was to place national banking associations on the same
level with State banking institutions with respect to
powers necessary to meet the drain of funds.

But the rush for cash had descended upon the banks
with such speed and in such volume that efforts to meet
it necessarily dealt with exigencies only. Financial
conditions were "spotty" and there was no uniformity
of strength across the country which could offset the
impact of a national stampede for cash. President
Roosevelt's proclamation declaring a national bank
holiday became effective March 6, and placed all banks
on the same uniform level in the face of the crisis. He
acted under the unrepealed war powers granted to
President Wilson by the Act of October 6, 1917, giving
the President plenary powers over "any transactions in
foreign exchange, and the export, hoarding, melting, or
earmarkings of gold or silver coin or bullion or currency . . . "; and providing for a fine of $10,000
and/or imprisonment for not more than ten years for
a violation of the Act. The President's order closed the
banks from March 6 to the 9th; and by further order
on the 9th, was continued "in full force and effect until
further proclamation by the President." Practically
every kind of banking transaction was prohibited; except that, with the approval of the President, the Secretary of the Treasury was empowered to permit banking
institutions to resume banking functions, to arrange for
the issuance of clearing house certificates (a form of

scrip currency), and to provide for the acceptance and separate handling of new deposits, as his discretion dictated, and under such regulations as he might prescribe. The majority of the banks had been perfectly solvent for all ordinary financial purposes except a "run" (which by the very nature of the banking business, no bank as at present constituted could survive); and the purpose of the directions to the Secretary of the Treasury was to enable these solvent banks to reopen as quickly as possible.

In his message to the new (73d) Congress on March 9, 1933, the President asked for legislation "to give the executive branch of the Government control over banks . . ., authority . . . to open such banks as have already been ascertained to be in sound condition . . . and authority to reorganize and reopen such banks as may be found to require reorganization to put them on a sound basis." He also asked for amendments to the Federal Reserve Act to provide for whatever additional currency may be required in the emergency. The President declared his belief that the legislation requested "will also mark the beginning of a new relationship between the banks and the people of this country." On the same day, Public Act No. 1 (H.R.1491), giving the President all that he had requested, was passed by both Houses of Congress. The President approved of the bill in the evening and it went into immediate effect. It was emergency legislation with very few questions asked. It was a fairly conclusive answer to a criticism of long standing, namely, that democratic government is at best a slow, clumsy, and inflexible process in the face of modern conditions.

THE EMERGENCY BANKING ACT

Title I of the Act confirmed everything that the President had done under existing legislation and upon his own initiative. It broadened by amendment that part of the wartime Act of October 6, 1917, giving plenary power to the President "During time of war or during any other period of national emergency declared by the President, . . . " To Section 11 of the Federal Reserve Act as amended, it added a new subsection empowering the Secretary of the Treasury to require the surrender of all gold coin, bullion, and gold certificates in exchange for an equivalent amount of any other form of coin or currency issued under the laws of the United States; and provided a penalty against all who failed to comply. It placed the National Banking System and the Federal Reserve System under the control of the President.

In a manner such as to preserve the large powers of the President and of certain other officials, Title II authorized the Comptroller of the Currency to appoint conservators for national banking associations anywhere in the United States, and any bank or trust company in the District of Columbia. The office of a conservator is practically the same as that of a receiver, but the manner of the appointment of conservators, the powers they possess, and the procedure under which they operate, are all designed to provide more flexible and speedier administration of the institutions committed to their care than is customary in the usual receivership process. The conservator's primary purpose, as the name implies, is to conserve the assets of a bank for the benefit of the depositors, the creditors, and the stockholders. To that end he has complete charge of the assets and business affairs of the bank. After examination and investigation, he may terminate the conservatorship and permit the bank to resume its functions under such regulations as he may prescribe. If the circumstances warrant it, he may approve and assist in any plan to reorganize a bank providing he is satisfied "that the plan of reorganization is fair and equitable to all depositors, other creditors and stockholders and is in the public interest. . . ." He may move toward the liquidation of any bank.

Title III is designed to strengthen the capital structure of the bank. It authorizes any national banking association, subject to certain conditions, to issue preferred stock "in such amount and with such par value" as shall be approved by the Comptroller of the Currency. A maximum dividend rate, cumulative, is fixed at 6 per cent per annum. The stock carries voting rights, and the holders are relieved from certain responsibilities usually attaching to bank stocks, such as, for example, assessments to restore impairments in the capital of the institution. The preferred stock has a prior lien over the common stock for dividends and upon liquidation. An important provision under this Title is that which permits the Secretary of the Treasury, with the approval of the President, to request the Reconstruction Finance Corporation to subscribe for

preferred stock of any national banking association or
any State bank or trust company in need of funds for
capital purposes, or to make loans to such institutions
for similar purposes.

Title IV amends the Federal Reserve Act so as to
provide Federal Reserve banks with additional currency in the form of "circulating notes" to the full face
value of "any direct obligations of the United States,"
or 90 per cent of the estimated value "of any notes,
drafts, bills of exchange, or bankers' acceptances" acquired from any member bank or any individual, partnership or corporation, and deposited with the Secretary of the Treasury. The provisions under this Title
are clearly intended to serve in the emergency only as
a means of assuring adequate currency, since the privileges granted thereunder cease when the President
declares that the emergency has terminated, or are
otherwise limited in time.

The foregoing constitutes the principal provisions of
the emergency banking Act. By an amendment passed
and approved on March 24, 1933, "any State bank or
trust company not a member of the Federal reserve
system" is brought within the purview of Title IV as
above described, ostensibly for the purpose of providing such institutions with an adequate supply of currency should the need arise.

EMERGENCY ACTIONS IN FINANCE

With this machinery at his disposal, the President
started it in operation by an Executive Order issued on
March 10, 1933. The Order permitted the Secretary

of the Treasury to allow member banks of the Federal Reserve System to perform any or all of their usual banking functions. It authorized State banking authorities to do the same with institutions under their jurisdiction. Certain safeguards were thrown around this resumption of banking facilities, and all transactions involving gold coin, gold bullion or gold certificates were either prohibited or strictly limited. Strict provision against hoarding of currency was ordered, and transactions in foreign exchange were limited to "legitimate and normal business requirements. . . ."

Following a brief press announcement respecting the technical difficulties and the proposed plans for reopening the banks, the President turned to the people of the country and addressed them over the radio on March 12, 1933. He explained banking procedure to them in amazingly plain and simple language. He explained the crisis and the steps taken to meet it. He reassured them with respect to the plans for a progressive reopening of banks, first in the Federal Reserve Bank cities of which there are about 250, and later in the smaller places. He affirmed the soundness of the new currency to be issued. He did not disguise the fact that some losses might be sustained. He took the people into his confidence and put the chances of success before them. "Let us unite in banishing fear," he said. "We have provided the machinery to restore our financial system; it is up to you to support and make it work."

Beginning with March 6, the Secretary of the Treasury promulgated a large number of regulations and a series of interpretations. In brief, they were designed to care for emergency conditions such as immediate business and personal requirements for funds in the handling of perishable foods, essential needs for wages and salaries, relief of distress, the clearing of checks, and so on. Later they authorized the reopening of Federal Reserve Banks, and other financial institutions under Federal supervision. Beginning with March 13, an orderly reopening of banks commenced in fact, the Federal and State authorities working in excellent unison, notwithstanding the degree of confusion and the immense technical difficulties involved in a dual and heterogeneous banking system. By March 25, 265 national banks with total deposits of approximately $350,000,000 had been placed in a position to open and were doing their normal banking business. By the middle of April approximately 80 per cent of the Federal Reserve member banks had reopened without restrictions, and about 70 per cent of the State banking institutions were doing business on an unrestricted basis. Commencing with the middle of March, currency, which had exceeded seven and a half billions of dollars at the peak of withdrawals, began to flow back to the banks, and, by the end of May, money in circulation was reduced to 5,876 millions of dollars. At the end of May, some 12,787 banks were reported to be in full operation without restrictions. It is estimated that they held approximately 90 per cent of the total moneys on deposit throughout the country. So far as the immediate, internal emergency was concerned, confidence was restored, and the crisis was ended.

But the experience left several serious problems for

solution. One of the most important was the relation between gold and the nation's business and financial structure. Much speculation surrounded the question whether or not the nation had abandoned the gold standard at the time the banking holiday was first proclaimed. The wording of the President's proclamation, of the emergency banking act, and of the regulations issued by the Secretary of the Treasury, allows much room for debate on this point.

The essential feature of the gold standard is the assured right of the exchangeability of the nation's currency for gold. When this right is impaired or denied the country can scarcely be said to be on the gold standard. From March 6 this right was certainly impaired in practice, even if not in law, by any strict interpretation of the acts and orders pertaining to gold. That is, the banks were either closed so that it was impossible to get gold; or when they did reopen, they were prohibited from paying out both gold and gold certificates.

But whatever doubts may have arisen, they were resolved by the Executive Order of the President on April 5, 1933, which prohibited the hoarding of gold and required the delivery of all gold coin, gold bullion and gold certificates into the Federal Reserve system on or before April 28, 1933. Minor exceptions were made in favor of such gold as may be required in industry, the professions and the arts, a personal allowance not to exceed $100, rare gold coins, and legitimately licensed quantities. By a further order on April 20, additional restrictions were applied, dealing principally with the export of gold under license. The Secretary of the Treasury followed these orders with a series of regulations making them effectual. All the previous orders pertaining to gold were merged in a more comprehensive order issued on August 29, 1933, which, except under strict license, prohibited all private holdings or transactions in gold, and provided a fine and/or imprisonment for all violations of the order. A suit, ostensibly to test the law, is now in progress.

Countless public and private obligations in the past and up to the spring of 1933 provided payment in gold, or gold coin, "of the present standard of value." It is estimated that obligations of this character total approximately one hundred billions of dollars. By a Joint Resolution effective June 6, 1933, the right to require payment of such obligations in gold was "declared to be against public policy," was prohibited as to all future obligations, and could be satisfied completely by payment, "dollar for dollar, in any coin or currency, which at the time of payment is legal tender for public and private debts." It is, therefore, this problem of what will be done about gold, both in relation to business agreements and to the currency system of the country, that may yet have to find a different solution —in a larger recovery program—than the one which emerged from the crisis and which has been described above.

The second problem of importance has to do with more than 5,000 banks which were closed during the crisis and were not permitted to reopen at all. Approximately two billions of dollars remain tied up in these banks. Recently, steps have been taken to free a portion of these deposits. As this question, as well as the reorganization of the banking structure and the question of inflation, are more definitely a part of the long-term Recovery Program, they will be considered in detail under the appropriate heading in that connection.

The financial problems are by no means settled, but the immediate crisis was met and settled with such intelligence and despatch that even the severest critics appear willing to give some applause to the administration.

CHAPTER III

ECONOMY AND EFFICIENCY IN GOVERNMENT

BALANCING THE BUDGET

THE government budget is something everyone wants to balance—until he finds himself involved in the scales. Then somehow the idea becomes too complicated, and its attractiveness falls away. Budgets may be balanced by decreased expenditures or increased income or a little of both. No matter how it is proposed to be done there is stubborn resistance. Such considerations vexed the Hoover régime and tied the hands of all Congresses forced to face the issue. But throughout the post-war decade the issue had not become serious, primarily because ordinary receipts exceeded expenditures chargeable against them. Deficits commenced in 1931. In that year, ending June 30, 1931, expenditures (including public debt retirements approximating 440 millions of dollars) exceeded ordinary receipts by $902,-700,000. At the close of the next fiscal year on June 30, 1932, the deficit was $2,885,400,000. On March 4, when President Roosevelt took office, the government was faced with authorized expenditures (excluding sinking fund requirements) of approximately $3,158,-000,000 as against estimated income of $2,280,000,000 for the fiscal year 1933-1934.

President Roosevelt struck the keynote of the situation in his message to Congress four days after the session began. "Our government's house is not in order and for many reasons no effective action has been taken to restore it to order. . . . Too often in recent history liberal governments have been wrecked on rocks of loose fiscal policy. . . . The Members of the Congress and I are pledged to immediate economy. . . . The proper legislative function is to fix the amount of the expenditure, the means by which it is to be raised and the general principles under which the expenditures are to be made. The details of expenditure, particularly in view of the great present emergency, can be more wisely and equitably administered through the Executive."

Responding to this request for broad powers, the Congress passed the Economy Act to Maintain the Government Credit, and the law received the President's approval on March 20. Under Title I, with some exceptions, the law practically swept away twelve years of statutes relating to benefits payable to Spanish-American, World War, and other veterans. Setting broad categories of persons entitled to pensions, and fixing maximum and minimum rates in certain cases, it practically vested in the President complete authority to establish a new pension system.

After reposing such control in the President and agencies under his review, the Act insulated his actions against external attack in two ways: (1) in providing for the filing of claims for benefits, it was decreed that "When a claim shall be finally disallowed under this title and the regulations issued thereunder, it may not thereafter be reopened or allowed"; and (2) "All decisions rendered by the Administrator of Veterans' Affairs under the provisions of this title, or the regulations issued pursuant thereto, shall be final and conclusive on all questions of law and fact, and no other official or court of the United States shall have jurisdiction to review by mandamus or otherwise any such decision."

Title II reduces specific salaries and authorizes the President to fix all other government salaries in accordance with changes in the cost of living, reductions not to exceed 15 per cent. Practically all interference with the provisions under this title, by suit or otherwise, is cut off, except a test of its constitutionality. From the data introduced into the debates on the bill, it appears that savings ranging from 385 to 500 millions of dollars will result from the operation of the Act. From the nature of the Act, the savings constitute withdrawals, whether warranted or not, from the purchasing power of a considerable number of the people of the country, in favor of reduced taxation or public indebtedness.

On March 28, the President issued an order reducing practically all federal administrative salaries by 15 per cent effective April 1; and on July 5, this order was continued to January 1, 1934. By an executive order issued early in April, the President provided for the elimination of approximately four hundred millions of dollars in pensions and other benefits paid to veterans, effective July 1. The latter order raised such a storm

of protest from veterans, their friends, and Congress-
men, that a legislative attack on the free hand of the
President materialized in legislation designed to cushion
the economies and make them less drastic. Provisions
to that end were written into the appropriation bill for
executive and other independent offices (Public No.
78; H.R.5389) and finally approved by the President
on June 16, 1933. Through his power to bring about
economies and changes in the government administration, the President felt able to announce early in June
that a billion dollars savings would be realized on the
next year's budget.

His efforts to balance the budget were not aided by
reductions and curtailments in administrative agencies
alone. The beer bill, signed on March 22, was calcu-
lated to add about one hundred and fifty millions of
dollars to the federal income. The continuation and increase of the gasoline tax, the extension of levies under
the Revenue Act of 1932, the excise tax of 5 per cent
levied on dividends, the limitations on the deductibility
of losses on stock and bond transactions carried over
from previous years, the new capital stock tax, and the
5 per cent excess profits tax, were all expected to build
up the income side of the government's ledger.

Moreover, the ledger itself underwent a change in
that expenditures were to be divided into two classes,
and a sort of "double budget" was to be set up. The
plan had been under consideration for some time. The
President had indicated his opinion that just as wartime expenditures are funded over a long period of
time, the extraordinary expenditures of a peace-time

emergency should be treated in the same manner. Under such a system, the moneys being spent upon the various organizations of the Recovery Program, including activities definitely financed by bond issues, will be set up in something of a budget of their own. They will increase the public debt, but they will not affect the ordinary budget over each fiscal year. With these "capital" outlays out of the way, an attempt will then be made to make the ordinary receipts balance the ordinary, or "current," expenditures over the fiscal year. The difference between the budgets would be something like the difference recognized in corporation finance between current expenditures and capital outlays. President Roosevelt announced the change in time to have it go into effect beginning in July for the fiscal year 1934.

In view of this new bookkeeping system, it might be well to give some indication of the financial extent of the Recovery Program. From the enactments of the 1st Session of the 73d Congress (principally for the Recovery Program) the appropriations, authorizations, and contingent liabilities have been estimated as follows: direct appropriations and authorizations, $4,903,-000,000; and contingent liabilities, $6,050,000,000; or a total of $10,953,000,000. Most of this would fall within the extraordinary budget, or capital outlay account. It does not mean that the public debt will actually be increased by that amount, but that it may be. Many of the sums, such as the billions authorized for public works, may never be spent.

What is the budget situation to date? The deficit at

the close of the fiscal year, June 30, 1933, amounted to $1,791,200,000, showing the beginnings of a slight reduction. The deficit itself can scarcely be charged against the Roosevelt administration, however, since the latter had little control over the budget for the year then closed. Most of the expenditures and the income to meet them had been fixed by the prior administration. From a report just issued, covering the first quarter of the present fiscal year to September 30, 1933, internal revenue showed a gain of more than a quarter of a billion dollars over the same period last year, presumably on the old budget basis of comparison.

Many of the tax levies were designed to cease either when the budget was in balance or when the 18th Amendment to the Constitution was repealed, whichever was earlier. The fact that the 18th Amendment may be repealed before the year is out (some quip said that the "boys will be back in the drenches by Christmas") will enable the Roosevelt administration to put off for a time the embarrassing question: When is a budget balanced? Now that the liquor revenue laws will soon place their shoulders to the wheel, there should be no question but that the budget, under the new system, will balance. Some people will rest content on that achievement.

But there are others who will soon see that putting the whole public budget in a new dress does not change its face. Under the new system of bookkeeping, both the word "budget" and the word "balance" have been given a new significance which seems dangerously like postponing the fundamental question concerning the real issue in public finance. To the real issue involved in public finance, it makes little difference whether by "budget" we mean the old annual mixture of ordinary and extraordinary expenses as against total income, or whether we separate the ordinary from the extraordinary expenses (treating them as short-term and long-term expenditures) and likewise classify the income to meet them. The public will have to pay the full bill in either case.

This is not an attempt to condemn the Roosevelt dual budget system. That system has its advantages, and a good case can be made in its behalf. The same may be said of the old method of handling the budget. It is merely intended to point out that the real questions touching any kind of a budget for public finance— namely, what taxes to levy, what rates to apply, upon whom shall they fall, and so on—remain largely unanswered, and lie as much in the future for the Roosevelt régime as they had done for prior administrations in the post-war decade.

THE POLITICAL STRUCTURE AND GOVERNMENT ADMINISTRATION

The question of reorganizing the executive and administrative structure of the Federal Government was in the same dismal status prior to March 4 as the proposal to balance the budget had been. That is, everyone seemed to feel that the Government structure was growing clumsy, complicated and unwieldy—even bureaucratic—but no one seemed to be able to do anything about it. Dozens of departments, executive, and administrative agencies, were performing functions which might easily be fused in one, with a consequent gain in economy and efficiency. In some instances in the matter of Government purchases, several agencies were competing with each other with the result of raising the prices against each other and against the Government as a whole. Inefficiencies were patent, and the public paid the cost of waste in constantly mounting taxes.

Granting the profit system of economy in an age of mass production and technological unemployment, there is something to be said in favor of the growing number of federal employees and the multiplication of government agencies. Those who decry the mounting bureaucracies and the many attendant evils often do not think the thing through. It does not occur to them that as a result of the existing economic system, government employment has become a "service" industry into which thousands of persons, forced out or having no chance to get into the field of private "production," were poured from the same economic spillway that created the excessive number of bond salesmen, advertising writers, public relations counsellors, social workers, and the like.

This accounts in large measure for the stubborn resistance which is made to all attempts to reorganize the government. Reorganization means unemployment for thousands of government workers, and they simply have no other place to which they can go. The truth of this should be apparent from even a cursory consideration of the "prosperity" years. With industry going full blast (at least relative to effective demand) and with an admittedly large government bureaucracy, there still remained more than two million persons without jobs. Therefore, any scheme for the future, whether it is the Recovery Program or something else, will have to come to grips with the fundamental problem that lies back of such a situation; namely, the relationship between absolute productive capacity, the total number and quality of persons ready to be "gainfully employed," and effective demand. That is the larger problem of course; and it really concerns our whole economic system. More will be said about it later. It was only mentioned at this point on account of its influence on the previous abortive attempts to reorganize and simplify the government structure.

After much wrangling between Congress and the Executive, the 72d Congress granted President Hoover the right to go into the question of reorganization on his own initiative. But the grant came too late in his régime and there was a string tied to it. Under the provisions of Title IV of the Treasury and Post Office Appropriation Bill (Public No. 428; H.R. 13520; 72d Congress, 2d Session) approved March 3, 1933, the President was granted the right to investigate the organization of all executive and administrative agencies and to determine what changes would be necessary to effect the following purposes: (a) reduce expenditures; (b) increase efficiency; (c) group, co-ordinate, and consolidate executive and administrative agencies according to major functions; (d) reduce the number of such agencies by consolidations under a single head, and by abolishing such as were not necessary; (e) eliminate overlapping and duplication; (f) segregate regulatory agencies and functions from those of administrative and executive character. The mere enumeration of things to be investigated is enough to indicate the complexities that had been creeping into the government structure.

Then the Bill went on to list broad categories of sweeping changes which the President might make by Executive Order. The Order was then to be submitted to the Congress while in session and did not become effective until after the expiration of 60 calendar days after such transmission, unless Congress provided an earlier effective date. But there was a proviso to what seemed like a free hand. If Congress adjourned before the elapse of 60 calendar days from the time of the transmission of the Executive Order, such Order was not to become effective until 60 days after the next regular or special session of Congress opened. While the proviso did not wholly constitute a joker, it certainly limited the chances of speedy and effective action. The President would have had to have on hand, ready for the convening of the Congress, a complete scheme of government reorganization because time commenced to run against him as soon as the session opened. The President was assured of long waits between his ideas for government economy and efficiency and the chance to realize upon them.

But Title III of the Roosevelt Economy Act (previously cited in connection with the budget) altered

that situation. It amended Sections 407 and 409 of
Title IV of the Treasury and Post Office Appropriation
Act so as to leave out the proviso which would have
tied the President's hands. So long as the President
transmitted his orders to the Congress in session, such
orders would go into effect at the expiration of 60 days.
Moreover, there was no way by which Congress could
prevent the orders from becoming effective short of re-
pealing or modifying the law under which the President
had acted; and it was conceivable that the President
might veto any such attempt by Congress, making a
two-thirds vote necessary for effective congressional action. Here at last was a free rein, a break in the deadlock in which Congress had neither permitted the
President to effect changes nor had displayed the ability to make the changes itself.

The President took advantage of his prerogatives as
was expected of him when the Act was passed. But
the Congress was surprised and a little resentful when
he did act, not so much at his action perhaps but
rather because it appeared that he had delayed action
until near the close of the session when the press of
public business was almost too great for Congress to
give full consideration to any matter laid before it. In
an Order dated June 10, 1933, consisting of some
twenty-two sections, the President made some significant changes in the organization of the executive and
administrative agencies of the Government.

Under the heading of "Procurement," the "function
of determination of policies and methods of procure-

ment, warehousing, and distribution of property, facilities, structures, improvements, machinery, equipment, stores, and supplies exercised by any agency is transferred to a Procurement Division in the Treasury Department, at the head of which shall be a Director of Procurement." Under the same heading, a number of other changes and re-groupings were ordered. Major functions of agencies dealing with the "National Parks, Buildings, and Reservations" are consolidated in a single office in the Department of the Interior with a special director in charge.

Other changes under this title included the abolition of a number of special commissions. Practically all the functions of the Bureau of Prohibition are divided between a division of the Treasury Department and the Department of Justice. All disbursement of moneys is centered in a Division of Disbursement in the Treasury Department. The Department of Justice is given charge of all prosecutions and defenses touching upon claims and demands either in favor of or against the Government. Insular courts in China, the Panama Canal Zone, and the Virgin Islands, are transferred to the Department of Justice. The Shipping Board is abolished and its functions turned over to the Department of Commerce. Functions relating to immigration and naturalization are consolidated under a single Commissioner and centered in the Department of Labor. Control over appropriations is vested in the Director of the Bureau of the Budget. A number of officers are transferred from one department to another.

Economies are directly attained by such provisions as the cessation of compiling statistics of cities under 100,000 population, and 25 per cent cuts in payments for the following activities: vocational education and rehabilitation, agricultural experiment stations, coöperative agricultural extension work, and for the endowment and maintenance of colleges for the benefit of agriculture and the mechanic arts. With transfers and consolidations, the original agencies are abolished and their personnel "separated from the service of the United States." The Order makes a number of other changes in the executive and administrative agencies of the Government. By an earlier order the Federal Farm Board was abolished and all the agricultural credit agencies were centered in the Farm Credit Administration.

On the other hand, a whole new structure of executive and administrative agencies is being erected through the medium of government "corporations." To mention a few of the prominent ones, there are, besides the powerful Reconstruction Finance Corporation, the Federal Surplus Relief Corporation, the Commodity Credit Corporation, Federal Deposit Insurance Corporation, Home Owners Loan Corporation, and the Tennessee Valley Authority. In addition to these, there is quite a number of new special administrations and administrators, conservators, and coördinators. This is the proper place to consider these changes, since they affect the government structure and help to define its relation to the business, political, and social activities of the country at large. But inasmuch as most of these developments must be considered more in detail under other headings, it will be more helpful to delay the discussion as a whole and recur to them at a later point in this document.

CHAPTER IV

INDUSTRY AND TRANSPORTATION

INDUSTRY

WHEN President Roosevelt took office on March 4, the number of unemployed was estimated to be 12,-000,000 persons. In addition, untold numbers of "employed" persons were "sharing" their work with others, which meant that they worked only part of the time and suffered reductions in wages accordingly. It was no time to speculate upon the causes of the condition. It was a fact. It was contributing to an unprecedented increase of crime. It was the principal factor behind the increasing appearances of social unrest indicating a serious threat to the social structure, even as licks of flame in a smoky building portend a condition menacing the very existence of the edifice.

At the same time the press of conditions forced a savage competition within and between industries that depressed wages below a subsistence level, drove prices below the costs of production, threatened the quality of the product, and demoralized the processes of production and exchange. Under such circumstances only the hardest could survive; and the conditions of survival seemed to favor those who were the most ruthless, those who stooped to the worst practices, those who felt forced to destroy rather than be destroyed, in an economic struggle in which all the rules of fair play seemed to be suspended. The real menace of it all, recognized and feared by all who gave serious thought to the situation, was that even the victors might gain the ashes of defeat as the fruits of triumph in such a struggle.

Three years of distress served only to intensify the deplorable conditions. The clamor for further and more drastic action grew too great to be ignored. It took all sorts of forms and demanded all kinds of remedies. One program—supported by a substantial body of opinion—demanded a shorter work day and a shorter work week without any corresponding decrease in the wage rate or level. Another suggestion, equally well-supported, sought relief from destructive competition in some sort of a guarantee of fair competition, enforced by the weight of government power. Underlying all was the widespread belief that only a "planned" economy could meet the emergencies of the present and serve the needs of the future. Out of the coalescence of ideas, under the psychological tonic of the expectations of a "new deal," the National Industrial Recovery Act emerged. The NIRA (Public No. 67; H.R.5755, 73d Cong. 1st Sess.) was approved by the President on June 16, 1933.

The first section of the Act states the conditions that brought its passage, declares its purposes, and attempts to assure its constitutionality, as may be seen from the following excerpts: "A national emergency productive of widespread unemployment and disorganization of industry, which burdens interstate and foreign commerce, affects the public welfare, and undermines the standards of living of the American people, is hereby declared to exist. It is hereby declared to be the policy of Congress to remove obstructions to the free flow of interstate and foreign commerce . . . to provide for the general welfare . . . to induce and maintain united action of labor and management under adequate government sanctions and supervision, to eliminate unfair competitive practices, to promote the fullest possible utilization of the present productive capacity of industries, to avoid undue restriction of production (except as may be temporarily required), to increase the consumption of industrial and agricultural products by increasing purchasing power, to reduce and relieve unemployment, to improve standards of labor, and otherwise to rehabilitate industry and to conserve natural resources."

Title I concerns the organization of industry to effectuate the purposes of the Act which, in the words of the President, "was passed to put people back to work—to let them buy more of the products of the farms and factories and start business at a living rate again." Two situations are recognized: (1) "the emergency job," or immediate reëmployment on temporary minimum standards; and (2) "to plan for a better future for the longer pull."

The President is given a free hand to "establish such agencies," "to appoint . . . such officers and employees," to utilize such existing agencies, to make such regulations regarding them, and to delegate such of his functions and powers to them, as in his discretion may be necessary to carry out the purposes of the Act.

"Upon the application to the President by one or more trade or industrial associations or groups, the President may approve a code or codes of fair competition for the trade or industry or subdivision thereof . . ."; and upon his approval the provisions of the code shall be "the standards of fair competition for such trade or industry or subdivision thereof." The associations or groups are to be truly representative of the trades or industries, and must not impose restrictions on admission to membership. No code shall be designed to promote monopolies, eliminate or oppress small enterprises, or operate to discriminate against them.

In the formulations of codes, adequate opportunity to be heard is assured to all interested parties. Sufficient flexibility is provided for the codes to meet diverse conditions in industrial and business organization. To aid further in carrying out the policy of the Act, "The President is authorized to enter into agreements with, and to approve voluntary agreements between and among, persons engaged in a trade or industry, labor organizations, and trade or industrial organizations, associations, or groups."

The present century, more particularly the years since 1910, witnessed the drawing together along the lines of common interests, through trade and other associations, of almost all of our 2,000 industries. These groups were designed to promote and protect the mutual interests of their constituent units, work out their common problems, and improve their service to the public. Similarly, other organizations—labor groups, professional bodies, consumers' associations, and the like—had been in the process of formation during the same years, and were also seeking to advance the interests of their constituents. Although all of these groups had accomplished many worthwhile objects both for their own members and for the general public, they fell far short of achieving the larger purposes expected of them. The National Industrial Recovery Act recognizes the existence of these historical movements toward group solidarity, operates to accelerate the process, and by government encouragement, protection, supervision, and control, seeks to weld them all into a vast unified structure designed to bring about their self-regulation for an equitable balance of their several interests to the end that greater efficiency, the elimination of abuses, and higher standards, will be achieved primarily in the service and for the good of the whole American people.

To insure further the objects of the Act, the President, on his own motion, may impose a code of fair competition where none exists, and it will have the same force and effect as codes voluntarily formulated by industry itself. He has the power also "to license business enterprises" under such regulations as he may prescribe whenever the conditions warrant such action. Whenever such a license shall be required, no person shall "engage in or carry on any business, in or affecting interstate or foreign commerce" without it, on penalty of a fine "of not more than $500," or imprisonment of "not more than six months, or both," with each day such violation continues being deemed a separate offense. Through the Federal Trade Commission and the several district courts of the United States, violations of the codes of fair competition are to be prevented and restrained. Other means of enforcement emerge from the President's power to require the filing of information, to prescribe rules and regulations, to make investigations, and to take any proper action necessary to effectuate the purposes of the Act.

In addition to the implied right to define and fix the conditions for the self-regulation of industries and trade, the codes are required to set the maximum hours of labor, the minimum rates of pay, and other conditions of employment, as shall be approved or prescribed by the President. To insure this, as well as the more important right for labor to organize itself, section 7 (a) of Title I of the Act provides that:

"Every code of fair competition, agreement, and license approved, prescribed, or issued under this title shall contain the following conditions: (1) That employees shall have the right to organize and bargain collectively through representatives of their own choosing, and shall be free from the interference, restraint, or coercion of employers of labor, or their agents, in the designation of such representatives or in self-organization or in other concerted activities for the purpose of collective bargaining or other mutual aid or protection; (2) that no employee and no one seeking employment shall be required as a condition of employment to join any company union or to refrain from joining, organizing, or assisting a labor organization of his own choosing; and (3) that employers shall comply with the maximum hours of labor, minimum rates of pay, and other conditions of employment, approved or prescribed by the President."

Subject to the approval of the President, employers and employees may fix the maximum hours of labor, minimum rates of pay, and other conditions of employment, by mutual agreement. Where this has not been done, the President has the power to do it upon his own initiative, and the limited code of fair competition so prescribed has the same force and effect as if voluntarily established by the industries themselves.

Two distinct benefits are assured by the Act. Either upon his own motion or at the instance of any group which has complied with the provisions of the Act, the President may, in accordance with procedures under his control, place fees upon, restrict, or forbid, except under regulations and license, the importations of any article or articles which "render ineffective or seriously endanger the maintenance of any code or agreement" under the Act. The decision of the President as to the facts is conclusive. In addition to this protection from the effects of importations from abroad, industry is privileged to enjoy a more positive benefit within the domestic field. So long as the law is in effect and for sixty days thereafter, "any code, agreement, or license approved, prescribed or issued and in effect under this title, and any action complying with the provisions thereof taken during such period, shall be exempt from the provisions of the antitrust laws of the United States."

Although ostensibly dealing with "transportation," a

special section affects the production and marketing of petroleum. This section authorizes the President to initiate proceedings before the Interstate Commerce Commission to control the operations and fix reasonable, compensatory rates for the transportation of petroleum and its products by pipe lines; and "to divorce from any holding company any pipe-line company controlled by such holding company which pipe-line company by unfair practices or by exorbitant rates in the transportation of petroleum or its products tends to create a monopoly." The President is authorized "to prohibit the transportation in interstate and foreign commerce of petroleum and the products thereof produced or withdrawn from storage in excess of the amount permitted to be produced or withdrawn from storage by any State law or valid regulation or order prescribed thereunder, by any board, commission, officer, or other duly authorized agency of a State." A penalty for violations is prescribed.

By another section, containing something of a "saving clause" on other legislation, co-ordination is assured with the administration of the Agricultural Adjustment Act. Individuals pursuing the vocation of manual labor and selling or trading the products thereof and persons marketing or trading the produce of their farms do not come under the provisions of the NIRA. The President's power to "license business enterprise" is limited in time to "one year after the date of the enactment of this Act or sooner if the President shall by proclamation or the Congress shall by joint resolution declare that the emergency recognized by section 1 has ended";

while, except for the same circumstances, the whole of the Title I ceases to be in effect two years after the enactment of the law. Titles II and III deal with subjects which will be treated in another section of this document.

The foregoing constitutes the major provisions for the organization and conduct of industry, trade, and labor. Machinery designed to carry this legislation and the regulations issued in pursuance thereof into effect has been created; and is still being created, the process of forming administrative agencies presenting a state of flux because of the new problems constantly arising in connection with organization. The process has crystallized sufficiently, however, to permit a tentative summary of the administrative structure. It appears to have two parallel lines of development which are inter-related and coördinated at a number of points. The one is the general development which may be said to embrace the whole structure. The other is a development within the general structure—complementary to it—which seems to be designed to achieve immediate, organizational purposes and to meet the problems arising from such an activity.

It is obvious from the previous outline of the legislation that, within the purview of the whole Act, the President is the central, controlling, absolute authority. In his statement at the signing of the Act, he made two major appointments: General Hugh Johnson, as Administrator of the National Recovery Administration (hereinafter called the NRA); and a special Industrial Recovery Board under the chairmanship of the

Secretary of Commerce.* The former is something of a general manager having jurisdiction over the whole re-employment program. The latter appears to operate as a board of directors. The two operate as the central directorate.

Three major advisory boards have been created to assist the three principal interests concerned in the NIRA. An Industrial Advisory Board, appointed by the Secretary of Commerce, is charged with the responsibility of seeing to it that every affected industrial group is fully represented in an advisory capacity; and any interested group will be entitled to be heard through representatives of its own choosing. This board is expected to do everything legitimately within its power to assist employers to place their interests before the NRA. A Labor Advisory Board, appointed by the Secretary of Labor, is charged with a similar responsibility respecting "every affected labor group, whether organized or unorganized." A Consumers' Advisory Board, appointed by General Johnson, occupies a position of like responsibility respecting "the consuming public."

Because of the difficulties involved in any adjustment of industry and labor to the framework of a new system, some means of composing differences was believed indispensable to avoid discontent, irritation, and aggressive action on the part of the two great interests concerned. Upon the recommendation of the Industrial and Labor Advisory Boards, a National Board of

* For various reasons, only the structure of the organization will be described, omitting the names of the personnel as a rule.

Arbitration (or Mediation Board) was appointed by the President. Composed of seven members, it seeks to function as a central tribunal of balanced interests. Granting the broad and liberal views of practically all of its members, the Board is divided roughly among three men who understand and sympathize with labor's interests; three men who might be said to incline toward the interests of trade and industry; and one United States Senator. The Board is designed to consider, adjust and settle differences and controversies which may arise through differing interpretations of the President's re-employment agreement. It functions something like an economic supreme court for labor and industry, having original jurisdiction in certain classes of difficulties, and exercising a sort of appellate jurisdiction in matters referred to it by district and local mediation boards established throughout the country. Except that they act locally and for circumscribed districts, these minor boards perform much the same functions as does the major tribunal at Washington.

The structure just described constitutes one phase of development. It is the principal one and may be expected to remain the permanent structure as long as the new industrial system operates. The other phase of development is largely temporary in character. Although falling within the principal structure, and coordinating with it at many points, this second phase of development deals primarily with the President's re-employment agreement.

Recognizing that many difficulties would attend and

delay the formulation of codes of fair practice, and believing that there was an impelling necessity to put the principles of the NIRA into immediate operation, the device of the President's re-employment agreement was formulated. This is a voluntary agreement between the President and employers and other groups concerned, pending the adoption of a code affecting them. Briefly, this agreement so regulates the employment of persons under 16 years of age as to eliminate what is commonly understood as "child labor"; it sets maximum working hours for various classes of employees; it fixes minimum rates of pay in accordance with the categories of employees both with respect to an occupational and a geographical basis; it seeks to hold down the prices of merchandise by admitting only such increases as the costs under the Recovery Program necessitate; it pledges support to such establishments as have come within the NRA; it provides for adjustments against hardships arising out of the Recovery Program; and it expires when the person or group signing the agreement comes within the operation of a permanent code. It has been called a "Blanket Code" which, as a temporary measure, any employer or any industry may sign and place in operation.

The machinery established to bring about the signing and operation of these agreements constitutes the second, the subsidiary, phase of development to which reference has been made. It consists of a Blue Eagle Division of the NRA and comprises a Washington Headquarters and a field staff of 26 District Boards. The District Boards "advise" and "report" upon the

problems and progress of the re-employment agreements. State Recovery Boards, composed of volunteers
from among persons prominent in each State, perform
similar functions in each State. They are assisted by a
field staff known as State Recovery Councils who
"recommend," suggest, and "request" on matters
touching the re-employment agreements. Finally,
NRA Local Committees carry the same process into
the smallest local units throughout the nation. Except
for the Administration staff at the Washington Headquarters, none of these bodies has any power to "pass
upon" matters that come within its purview. The
principal object of this subsidiary organizational structure is to secure the widest possible operation of the
President's re-employment agreement.

Because both the principal line of development and
this subsidiary development have a single, paramount
object to achieve—namely, the organization of the entire business structure of the nation in accordance with
the principles and plan laid down in the NIRA—they
co-ordinate and sometimes appear to merge at a number of points. For example, NRA Local Committee
Chairmen have been instructed, in a communication
direct from General Johnson, to create "Compliance
Boards." These, which are to be composed of seven
persons representative of employers, employees, and
consumers, together with a legal member and a person
who is a prominent member of the local community,
are designed to deal with maladjustments and complaints in connection with the President's re-employ-

ment agreements. In practice they perform most of the functions expected of local mediation boards contemplated as part of the supporting structure for the National Board of Arbitration at Washington. It may reasonably be said that they are now so considered in fact. There are many other points of contact between the two lines of development.

As the function for which this temporary structure was designed to perform is discharged, there will be a drawing together of the two lines of development. It will be in the direction of the absorption of the lesser, the temporary, organization into the major or permanent structure. Some duties will be discarded, others will be enlarged, and co-ordination will bring about a single, well-knit, organizational structure through which the industrial life of the nation will be supervised and administered. The whole will be assisted by the vast fact-finding agencies of the Federal Government which now draw, from every section of the country and from every part of the world, the information required for life and work in the amazing complex of American civilization.

Penetrating both these phases of development are the activities of General Johnson and his staff, constituting the National Recovery Administration proper. For almost four months this was an anomalous unit and little was known about its structure. It appeared to be nothing more than a staff—a collection—of men acting as liaison officers, organizers, co-ordinators, "trouble shooters," and general assistants to the

smoother operation of the entire structure. It is practically that today, although it has now emerged with a
structure of its own.

In due course, it will consist of five divisions, each
a distinct unit of its own, with legal advisors, technical
experts, industrial, labor, and consumers' advisors, and
research and planning departments. These divisions
reflect a classification of American industry into broad
categories. The First Division embraces the extractive
industries but also includes automobiles, shipping, and
related industries. The Second Division deals with
construction and machinery. The Third with chemi-
cals, leather and allied manufactures; and the Fourth
with trades, services, textiles, and clothing. Each division has a chief administrator and a number of deputies.

The Fifth Division, now headed by General Johnson
himself, will be known as the Compliance Division.
Under it a regional code compliance system for operation throughout the nation will be set up. This division has charge of all complaints of violations of the
codes and the President's re-employment agreements.
Through its own machinery and a National Compliance
Board consisting of one member from the Industrial
Advisory Board, one member from the Labor Advisory
Board and the National Compliance Director, it will
attempt to conciliate and adjust the differences and
complaints arising out of codes and agreements; and, if
unsuccessful, it will refer such cases to the Federal
Trade Commission or the Attorney General for enforcement under the provisions of the NIRA and the
regulations made pursuant thereof.

Within the scope of the legislation previously outlined, and through the creation of the administrative
structure just described, the major part of the industrial life of the nation has been brought under a set of
standards of conduct. This was done by codes of fair
practice for specific industries and interests, by the
President's re-employment agreements, and a miscellaneous group of agreements which are modifications
of the President's blanket code. The NRA prepared
some codes and assisted in the preparation of practically all others. Industries and trade associations
drafted their own codes and brought them to Washington for approval, and the President's re-employment
agreements, prepared at Washington, were carried
throughout the land and received back through the
medium of the post offices. Hundreds of hearings were
held under official auspices and thousands of conferences took place all over the country.

Nearly a thousand codes, agreements, and understandings will emerge from the effort to organize the
industrial life of the country. As time passes, and as
opportunity for reflection and experiment supersedes
the frenzied efforts to achieve immediate objectives, it
may be expected that the number of these codes and
understandings will be reduced, their forms stabilized,
and some more orderly structure embracing them
achieved. Moreover it is now clear that many of them
will have to undergo considerable alteration.

It is impossible to describe all these codes, or even
to present a single one in complete detail. Each one
has to be considered separately and against the back-

ground of the activity falling within its scope. In general, a code takes its basic authority from the NIRA and the regulations issued thereunder; it sets maximum hours and conditions of labor; it fixes minimum rates of pay; it abolishes "child labor"; it guarantees to labor the right to organize and to be represented by men of its own choosing; it sets standards under which the business of those coming within its jurisdiction must be conducted; it may provide for uniform methods of accounting, the making of reports, the use of plants, machinery and equipment; it may set up some supervising authority to regulate, control, and police the activities conducted under the code; and it usually provides for the alteration or amendment of its provisions. A code is something like a constitution for the industries grouped under it, by which they are expected to become self-regulatory and self-governing. It must not be overlooked that the whole code structure falls practically within the domain of the absolute power of the President of the United States so long as Congress sustains, and does not repeal or fundamentally alter, the NIRA.

It may appear that the whole effort was a harmonious process of organization. Those who have cast even a most cursory glance at the newspaper headlines during the past four months will know that such has not been the case. There were delays in forming codes, many of which were deliberate and reprehensible. There were attempts, one of which was successful, to avoid the mandatory provisions of the NIRA; while members of other groups followed the letter, and violated the spirit, of the principles behind the legislation and the President's program. Prices were sometimes advanced entirely without warrant. Many wage and hours of labor adjustments were altered against the clear intent of the program. In commenting upon violations of the spirit of the program, the President dignified the slang epithet of "chiselers," which seems to be well understood in American life. There were disputes within groups, such as labor organizations, members of trade associations, and the like, which had more to do with their own internal structure than with the Recovery Program of the nation. Finally, a small percentage of the nation's industries and employers, subject to organization under the NIRA refused to bring themselves voluntarily within the formal effort of the program.

Much of this confusion and many of these controversies are directly traceable to the speed and often to the wavering action of the organization itself; while the sensational display surrounding the introduction of the "Blue Eagle" threatened, at one time, to bring down upon the industrial program a storm of protest (principally against its boycott technique) and a wave of hysteria which sometimes characterizes certain stages of American mass action. General charges of regimentation and of "dictatorship" have persisted throughout the period of operations since March 4, and may not subside for some time to come. It is even possible that coming events will increase this outcry whether, upon sound thought, it is justifiable or not.

But the major effort of organization along the new lines appears to be over. A period of consolidation, of crystallizing the structure, of picking up the loose ends and straightening out the kinks, of strengthening it here and there, seems to have set in. It is likely to be followed by more determined efforts to enforce the legislation, the regulations, the codes, and the spirit of the program.

In addition to the means of enforcement contained in the NIRA and the action taken under its authority, as already noted, there is the threat of the withdrawal of the "Blue Eagle." This was an identification device granted to those who have been recognized as co-operators with the President through the codes, the re-employment agreements and otherwise. Posters bearing the special insignia were distributed through official procedure for display in the factories and shops. Replicas of it appear, either as stamps and labels, imprints or die impressions, upon almost all merchandise. "We Do Our Part" is the message they carry.

The implication behind the procedure was that those who did not display the "Blue Eagle" were "not playing the game"; and the implication became the basis upon which the people were exhorted, sometimes quite forcibly, to avoid doing business with such "noncoöperators." It was clearly a manifestation of the boycott technique which has its advantages and disadvantages. Except in rare cases, boycotts involving mass action are difficult to sustain for any length of time. For this reason it is reasonably safe to say that their use as an enforcement agency in connection with the Recovery Program will be discarded. In passing, it may be observed that the procedure undoubtedly contributed toward speeding up the acceptance of the President's re-employment agreements and the formulations of the codes; although the advisability of such haste is itself open to much sound criticism.

Aside from consolidation and a possible "wave" of enforcement which may be expected to ensue for the next several months, the principal problems will arise in connection with the standards set by the codes and agreements. The standards of hours and wages are questioned in many quarters and doubtless will have to undergo considerable modification on a broad front before they will contribute toward the realization of the principles behind the Recovery Program. No adequate mechanism for handling prices on a fundamental basis (except indirectly through the manipulations of gold and currency) has as yet appeared, except as in the oil and retail codes; and neither of them goes to the root of the price problem. So price is a problem for the future. Production itself—on which Henry Ford fired the opening gun by exercising the right to withdraw from society the means of production according as his own interests alone dictated—is also a problem for the future. These three are of paramount importance and, fundamentally, their solutions are still to be found. There are other problems of lesser consequence and a number of them are noted elsewhere in this document. All that can be said at the present moment on this industrial section of the Recovery Program is that much ground has been cleared, some parts of the foundations have been laid, the edifice is still to be erected, and its ultimate utility determined.

The principal measure of the Recovery Program dealing with transportation is the "Emergency Railroad Transportation Act of 1933." The legislation is manifestly experimental and is designed for temporary operation only. This is not to say that it will not leave permanent effects. It will. The laws—any laws—are rare which, when repealed or otherwise terminated, reinstate the *status quo*. The Act under discussion is no exception to the general rule. There is something of "salvage," something of "conservation"—"a clearing of the ground in preparation"—about the Act. It is designed to meet a fairly specific and narrow set of conditions; and does not pretend to go to the root of transportation problems in the larger sphere.

A revolution throughout the whole field of transportation has been going on since the World War. To those not directly interested in transportation, the revolutionary character of the developments was obscured by the revel in "prosperity." Moreover, the transitions were economic, of a subtle, silent kind unaccompanied by the usual fanfare associated with "revolutionary" changes. Some "prosperity" did spread over the railroads in the post-war decade, but compared to what was going on in other fields of transportation, it was little more than a thin veneer. Once entrenched as an absolute monarch of transportation, the railroads were assailed by a savage competition which became all the more formidable through the effects of a world-wide depression.

The assault upon the railroads came simultaneously from the air, on the surface, and underground. A few statistics of the situation up to the brunt of the depression will illustrate the nature of the attack. As late as 1926, passengers carried by airplane totaled only 5,782; but in 1930, the number carried exceeded 417,505. In the same period, mail carried by airplane rose from 810,855 to 8,324,255 pounds. In the air too, the thin strand of the electric power conduit, carrying energy produced from coal consumed at the mouth of the mine, combined with other factors of coal consumption severely to assail the picturesque railroad coal gondola. In 1920, motor vehicle registrations totaled only 9,231,941; but by 1930 they reached the enormous figure of 26,691,000. Railroad conductors, riding empty passenger and freight trains, saw the substance of their traffic in automotive vehicles streaming along the concrete highways parallelling the railroad tracks. Imperceptibly, but inexorably, the passenger automobile took passengers out of the railway coaches; and the trucks cut deep into railway freight revenues.

Inland waterway traffic more than doubled in the last decade; while transcontinental tonnage handled through the Panama Canal increased by more than six hundred per cent. Underground, thousands of miles of oil pipe-lines, stretching all the way from the Oklahoma fields to the doors of New York City, were laid down; while the sight of the familiar railroad oil tanker became a rarity. The intensity of the struggle was revealed by an executive of the American Petroleum Institute who observed: " . . . railroads might have controlled all the branches of this country's transportation system. . . . But unfortunately for themselves, in view of developments, they chose another course. They adopted first the attitude of opposition to any possible rival. . . . Now rivals are inclined to thrive on opposition . . . particularly when the rivals offer something the public wants and which the railroads do not provide. . . . It is unfortunate for the railroads but the law of the survival of the fittest often applies as well to industries as to nature, and that industrial history proves the truth of the Rotarian motto, 'He profits most who serves best.' " Perhaps such a view was an extreme one, but it indicated clearly that the railroads were on the defensive along a broad front and that they were without good generalship.

Other factors were operative too—the burden of taxes, the complex of state regulatory laws, the antitrust legislation which needs no amplification here— but when the smoke of the battle lifted at the close of the decade, the railway operating revenues of class I railroads had fallen from $6,360,423,213 in 1923 to $3,161,928,659 in 1932; revenue ton-miles from 412 billion to 234 billion; and passenger-miles from 38 billion to 17 billion. During the same period, the average number of employees fell off from 1,857,674 to 941,544, the number in February, 1933; and the end is not yet in sight. Tragic as all this was to the railroads, it was more so to life insurance companies, mutual savings banks, commercial banks, educational, philanthropic, and religious institutions, hospitals and other public or semi-public agencies, which together had approximately six and a half billions of dollars invested in railroad securities upon which the return was threatened.

It should not be inferred that the life has been beaten out of the railroads. They are down, but not out. The railroad mileage in the United States today is about 250,000 miles. Railroads have a definite function to perform, and it is of such a character that it may never be wholly taken away from them. But the above account offers a glimpse of the conditions presented to the Congress when they commenced to consider the "Emergency Railroad Transportation Act of 1933."

The railroads appeared to be in a state of rout, and the 1933 Act was designed to aid them to collect and consolidate their forces. Here and there in the Act some measure of direct relief is made available to them. The Act creates the office of Federal Coördinator of Transportation who is appointed by the President, by and with the advice and consent of the Senate, or designated by the President from the membership of the Interstate Commerce Commission (the I. C. C.). The Coördinator is directed to divide the lines of the carriers into three groups—an eastern group, a southern group and a western group. In each group a regional coördinating committee, consisting of five regular members selected by the carriers, and two special members selected in such manner as the Coördinator may approve, is created.

Title I of the Act envisages three broad purposes: (1) to encourage and promote or require action on the part of the carriers, which will (a) reduce duplications of services and facilities, and permit joint use of terminals and trackage; (b) control allowances, accessorial services, and the charges for them; (c) avoid other wastes and preventable expenses; (2) promote financial reorganizations and improve carrier credit; and (3) "provide for the immediate study of other means of improving conditions surrounding transportation in all its forms and the preparation of plans therefor."

The achievement of the first of these purposes is left to the carriers themselves operating voluntarily through the regional committees set up under the Act. Standing alone there is nothing important about such an arrangement since the carriers can take such action under previous law. Something much more positive was necessary, and the Act supplied it. If the carriers, acting severally or through joint action of the committees, should be unable for any reason to accomplish the results desired, the committees may enlist the aid of the Coördinator who is empowered to "give appropriate directions . . . by order." The Coördinator may conceivably suggest action on any matter upon his own initiative, but he has no direct power to act in this respect, unless the ambiguous phraseology of the latter part of section 6 (a) could be construed to give him such a right. Orders issued by the Coördinator are required to be made public and do not go into effect for 20 days after publication. Any interested party (practically in the widest sense) dissatisfied with any order of the Coördinator may, at any time prior to the effective date of the order, file a petition for review with the I. C. C., which has the power to issue something like an "injunction" suspending the order pending a full hearing. The direction that the I. C. C. must expedite the hearing whenever it suspends an order seems to confirm the injunctive character of the proceedings. Moreover, the I. C. C. may confirm the order, set it aside, or re-issue it in modified form.

The Coördinator is directed to confer freely with the coördinating committees of the carriers. He has the right to request the carriers, the committees, the subsidiaries, and the I. C. C. to furnish him such information and reports as he may desire; and of even greater importance, both the Coördinator and the I. C. C. shall at all times have access to all accounts, records, and memoranda of the carriers and subsidiaries. Jurisdictional, judicial and other powers contained in the Interstate Commerce Act, as amended and supplemented, are extended to the Commission for the purposes of Title I of the 1933 Act; while persons subpœnaed or testifying are accorded the rights and are subject to the obligations of the same prior legislation.

Provisions are made for the creation of labor committees for each regional group of carriers. The coördinating committees and the Coördinator are charged with the duty to give reasonable notice to, and to confer with, the appropriate regional labor committees whenever the interests of employees are affected. Provision is made against any drastic reduction in the num-

ber of employees in the service of carriers; and the
Coördinator is directed to set up "regional boards of
adjustment" whenever and wherever necessary to settle
controversies arising under the Act between carriers
and employees. Just compensation must be paid by
the carriers for property losses and expenses imposed
upon employees by reason of enforced transfers from
one locality to another. Carriers are required to comply with provisions protecting labor as set forth in the
Railway Labor Act and in certain provisions of the
bankruptcy laws as amended.

An attempt to achieve the second purpose of Title
I is provided for in section 15 of the Act which states:
"The Commission shall not approve a loan to a carrier
under the Reconstruction Finance Corporation Act, as
amended, if it is of the opinion that such carrier is in
need of financial reorganization in the public interest:
Provided, however, That the term 'carrier' as used in
this section shall not include a receiver or trustee." At
the hearings held on the bill before its enactment, it
was brought out that this section might aid materially
in bringing about the much-needed reorganizations of
the capital structures of some of the roads. It was also
pointed out, however, that a carrier who could qualify
for a loan under this section would be likely to be
soundly organized and not in need of reorganization.
Certainly, the Coördinator has no direct power to force
reorganizations, but it is reasonable to infer that his
influence, aided by the requirements of this section for
the approval of loans, may bring about several of them.
If the section does little else, it may prevent the pour-

ing of public moneys into the enormous sinkhole of swollen and unsound capital structures.

The first two purposes above discussed are aimed to fill the "salvage" and "conservation" conceptions of Title I of the Act. They are likely to be far more beneficial to the carriers and the bond and stockholders than to labor or the country's transportation system. Many of the economies and much of the co-operation envisaged by the Act may go a long way toward the obliteration of the rivalries and jealousies between carriers which in the past have led to enormous waste, duplication of facilities, and destructive competitive practices. In this, there will be some gain to the public which had to pay the bill. The reorganizations of capital structures would also go a long way toward relieving the strain of a top-heavy structure; and if there are sacrifices for creditors and security-holders here and there, the process is not likely to be harsh. But it should be clearly recognized that some groups are going to be affected by operations carried out under the Act. Labor cannot escape some effects. Shippers will find themselves paying for many services and facilities which, formerly, they received free as a by-product of the rivalries among the carriers. Communities may expect the curtailment of some of their railroad services, which, at least in some cases in the past, has amounted to a tragedy. It is to be hoped that the character of the Coördinator, the exercise of his authority, the right to appeal to the I. C. C., and the preservation of the right to appeal to the courts as is now provided in the Interstate Commerce Act, will all operate to soften the effects of the curtailments likely to follow from this Act.

The provisions for carrying out the third purpose of the Act may come to have enormous significance for the transportation system of the country as a whole, or it may not amount to anything at all. This rests with the Coördinator. Under section 13 of Title I, he is charged with the duty "to investigate and consider means . . . of improving transportation conditions throughout the country, including cost finding in rail transportation and the ability, financial or otherwise, of the carriers to improve their properties and furnish service and charge rates which will promote the commerce and industry of the country and including also the stability of railroad labor conditions and relations"; and from time to time to make recommendations looking toward legislation to achieve such ends. This is the "clearing of the ground" section of the Act. The country has long awaited a unified, nation-wide transportation system, but this can never come about until the railroads bring themselves abreast of the times.

The wording of the first part of the section seems to contemplate a broad study in the field of transportation, and Mr. Joseph B. Eastman, Commissioner of the I. C. C. (now Coördinator), in his testimony before the Congressional Committees, seems to take that view of his task. He said, "I regard this portion of the bill as perhaps the most important of all. The transportation of the country is in a period of grave unsettlement pending important changes. New transportation agencies have appeared on the scene in great force. It is a period of strife, confusion, and instability. The proper place for each of these agencies must be found and in some way they must be coördinated and welded into a well-knit whole, into a transportation system operating much more nearly as a unit without cross purposes and all manner of lost motion."

With all of this there should be no dispute; but when Mr. Eastman (as well as this section of the Act under consideration) appears to imply that a unified transportation system may be brought about only through the agencies of the railroads as a nucleus, he is underestimating the magnitude of the task and the strength of opposing forces. Such an implication as is here observed does seem to follow from the following testimony: "It seems probable that to bring about such a result [a unified transportation system, including 'new transportation agencies' . . . on the scene in great force] the railroads must not only operate with maximum efficiency and economy but also change their methods of operation and service and their types of equipment in important respects and utilize motor vehicles and perhaps water and air carriers as auxiliaries to a much greater extent than at present."

By all means the country needs a coördinated transportation service, embracing a meshed system of land, air, and water carriers, but effort to bring this about solely through the exercise of administrative powers favoring the railroads as a nucleus is extremely dubious and threatens to precipitate a ruinous war between existing transportation agencies for supremacy. Unification ought to be brought about through an impartial study of all forms of transportation and through blanket legislation covering the whole, coming from a national body empowered to do the entire job, and not through a Coördinator of the railroads alone. Under the 1933 Act, the Coördinator would have enough to do, and the most he should be permitted to do, is to help to prepare the railroads for their place and function in a nation-wide transportation system.

Title II of the Act consists principally of amendments to the Interstate Commerce Act. It makes possible and lawful consolidations and mergers of railroad properties which, although contemplated by the Transportation Act of 1920, were never effected. It brings corporations controlling railroads, but not themselves carriers, within the purview of the Act. It seeks to prevent subterfuges, through holding companies and other devices, by which public supervision and control are rendered ineffective against glaring abuses.

The Act is not without substantial benefits to the carriers. The coördinating committees have a rare opportunity to achieve far-reaching results. Through the Coördinator, they will have the benefit of a highly skilled guidance in dealing with a mass of inter-related problems. They will have the aid of his positive powers of speedy action on important questions. Through the repeal of the "recapture" clause as provided in Title II, they will be relieved of accrued obligations of more than three hundred millions of dollars which had appeared to strain railroad credit to the breaking point. Through the orders and acts of the Coördinator, and

upon certain proceedings before the I. C. C., carriers
will be relieved from the operation of the antitrust
laws; and what is believed to be of greater significance,
from "all other restraints or prohibitions by law, State
or Federal, other than such as are for the protection of
the public health or safety. . . ."

Such a sweeping exemption as this last one, even
though the State authorities will be afforded full hearings, may prove to be very unwise in practice. For the
moment, no judgment can be expressed concerning it,
other than that liberalizing provisions of law, couched
in such broad and general terms as the one under discussion, are almost always harmful to the public interest in the long run.

The Act is substantially a "Carriers' Act." It has
nothing to do with lowering rates of railroad transportation, the matter of rates being left where it is now,
with the I. C. C. It will not aid labor materially, and
may even have adverse effects on railroad employees.
There is very little of direct benefit to the general
public, although the security holders and the creditors
are certain to gain by the Act. The railroads were like
a defeated army in disordered retreat, without competent or intelligent leadership notwithstanding the
ridiculously high salaries paid to many of their officials.
Yet this could apply with equal or greater force to
many fields outside of transportation. This Act has
intervened to give them a breathing spell, to afford
them a chance to collect and conserve their forces, to
give them an opportunity to stabilize and strengthen
their organizations; all with the help of a public offi-

cial and a generous government dispensation. If they do these things without delay, if they do them without caprice or subterfuge, if they make the most of the opportunity to prepare themselves for a truly coöperative part in an efficient transportation system, then any sacrifices temporarily demanded from special groups or running against the public interest may still be accepted with philosophical equanimity because they will be sacrifices of the lesser, to attain the greater, good.

CHAPTER V

AGRICULTURE

THE plight of the farmer has already been pointed out. His troubles centered mainly about two conditions: (1) the price disparities which in many cases gave him less than the cost of production of his products, and compelled him to pay disproportionate prices for the things he had to buy; and (2) his burden of indebtedness which operated to denude him of his personal property, deprive him of his home and farm by foreclosure, and cast him adrift in an unfamiliar environment where there was no job, no place for him. The Farm Relief Act (Public No. 10, H. R. 3835, 73d Cong. 1st Sess.) approved May 12, 1933, sought to meet and correct this situation.

Title I of the Act was addressed to the first of the two problems confronting the farmer. After summarizing the state of emergency that existed, its principal purpose was declared to be as follows: "To establish and maintain such balance between the production and consumption of agricultural commodities, and such marketing conditions therefor, as will reëstablish prices to farmers at a level that will give agricultural commodities a purchasing power with respect to articles that farmers buy, equivalent to the purchasing power of agricultural commodities in the base period. The base period in the case of all agricultural commodities except tobacco shall be the pre-war period, August 1909—July 1914. In the case of tobacco, the base period shall be the post-war period, August 1919—July 1929." This equality of purchasing power was to be brought about as rapidly as circumstances would permit; and in such a manner as not to raise the prices of agricultural commodities to the consumer above those in effect during the base period.

Cotton was an immediate problem when the Act was passed in the spring of the year. Planting seemed to be going forward totally oblivious of the fact that there was already in existence a world carryover of American cotton estimated at more than 12,000,000 bales. The farm price of cotton in June, 1932, had been 4.6 cents per pound, one of the lowest on record. In May, 1933, when the Act was approved, the price was 8.2 cents per pound, but still far below the level sought to be attained, especially in contemplation of the effect of the surplus stocks.

Part 1 of Title I dealt with this condition. After providing means for the Secretary of Agriculture to secure ownership or control of practically all cotton held by any other government departments, except the federal intermediate credit banks, the Secretary was authorized to enter into contracts with cotton growers under which they were required to reduce their 1933 production at least 30 per cent below that of the previous year. There was to be no increase in commercial fertilization per acre, and the land taken out of cotton production was not to be used for production for sale of any other nationally produced agricultural commodity or product. As an inducement to the grower, he was to have the option to buy cotton from the Secretary equal in amount to the reduction in production and at the average price paid for the cotton by the Secretary. The grower was protected against all responsibility or financial loss arising from the holding of the cotton. If the plan worked, it would bring about a reduction in cotton production while leaving the grower in no worse position—and possibly in a much better position—than if there had been no plan at all. In effect, the scheme embraced the idea of a subsidy in addition to all other factors which might operate to give a greater return to the cotton grower. The Secretary was authorized to employ the plan again in 1934; and directed to dispose of all the cotton in his control by March 1, 1936.

Part 2 deals with a number of basic agricultural commodities, and the Act designates them as wheat, cotton, field corn, hogs, rice, tobacco, and milk and its products. Here, the Secretary of Agriculture is empowered to do a number of things to reduce acreage, cut down the market supply, and thereby bring the price up to the desired level. He may enter into agreements with producers and provide rental or benefit payments in such amounts as are fair and reasonable. He may enter into marketing agreements with processors, associations of producers and others engaged in the handling of agricultural commodities, and such agreements are exempted from the operation of the antitrust laws. Loans from the Reconstruction Finance Corporation may be utilized in this connection.

More positive than these two powers, which merely envisage voluntary agreements, is the Secretary's power to issue licenses permitting processors, associations of producers, and others to engage in the handling of agricultural commodities, or any competing commodity or product thereof. This is a sweeping control over a wide area of production and marketing, and may even be so interpreted as to extend to fields other than those usually embraced within the term, agriculture. The power to license also carries with it, in specific terms, the additional authority to suspend or revoke licenses, and provides penalties for any violations. The Secretary also has the right to compel licensees to supply reports and information on quantities and prices of commodities, trade practices and charges, and to compel the keeping of systems of accounts.

To accomplish the purposes of the Act through the limitation and control of production and marketing, considerable funds will be necessary. Such revenue is to be provided for by processing taxes. Upon the Secretary's proclamation that rental or benefit payments are to be made with respect to any basic agricultural commodity, "a processing tax shall be in effect with respect to such commodity from the beginning of the marketing year therefor next following the date of such proclamation." The rate is to be determined by the Secretary, may be adjusted from time to time, so as to approximate "the difference between the current average farm price for the commodity and the fair exchange value of the commodity." Fair exchange value means a price giving the same purchasing power as that which had existed during the base period.

The tax is to be assessed against, and paid by, the processor "upon the first processing of the commodity," which is defined for each commodity. Consumers are to be protected from pyramiding of the tax and profiteering by information made public by the Secretary regarding: "(1) the relationship between the processing tax and the price paid to the producers of the commodity, (2) the effect of the processing tax upon prices to consumers of products of the commodity, (3) the relationship, in previous periods, between prices paid to the producers of the commodity and prices to consumers of the products thereof, and (4) the situation in foreign countries relating to prices paid to producers of the commodity and prices to consumers of the products thereof."

In the latest account of his stewardship, President Roosevelt illustrated one way in which this provision might operate, by citing the unconscionable price rise to $2.50 from $1.50 in the price of a cotton shirt, exacted by a "chiseler" under the excuse that the cotton processing tax (which amounted to 4¼ cents on the cotton in the shirt) had so increased the cost. These provisions for the protection and guidance of the public could become of inestimable value to the consumers, and it is to be hoped that they will be employed to the full and not permitted to atrophy in the Act.

The Secretary is given wide latitude over the em-

ployment of officers, employees, and agents. He has
the broad right to act by the flexible method of "regulations." He, or the Secretary of the Treasury, has the
sole right of final review on matters relating to rental
or benefit payments. Severe penalties seek to prevent
any official in the administration from speculating in
agricultural commodities and associated conditions.
Enforcement extends to the right to invoke proceedings under the Federal Trade Commission Act; and, in
Part 2, to action by the Attorney General in the United
States courts. An appropriation of $100,000,000 is
made available to the Secretary, as are all taxes imposed under the provisions of this Title of the Act. The
Act terminates whenever the President finds and pro-
claims that the national economic emergency in relation to agriculture has ended.

By supplementary provisions, abatement of the tax
may be made in certain cases, and exemptions may
relieve processors from taxes on all products used for
home consumption as well as for charitable distribution. Disadvantages in competition and excessive shifts
in consumption may be corrected by the right to levy
"compensating" taxes on the competing commodities.
A similar compensating tax, equal to the amount of the
processing tax in effect with respect to domestic processing, shall be levied on any imported article
processed or manufactured wholly or in chief value
from commodities which are taxed domestically under
the Act. A refund of the domestic processing tax is
to be allowed on exportations. Flour stocks are taxed
as if unprocessed; but retail stocks, excepting in ware-

house, are exempt. On existing contracts for the future delivery of products subject to tax, the vendee is required to pay the tax to the vendor who is responsible to the Commissioner of Internal Revenue for it, and may seek his aid in enforcing its collection. The Bureau of Internal Revenue is charged with the collection of the taxes and has the assistance of the provisions and penalties of existing revenue laws to aid it. In cases of hardship, taxpayers may have the benefit of a postponement not exceeding 90 days, and are eligible for loans from the RFC.

Results of this effort to reduce acreage, control production, and influence price require time because of the very nature of the commodities and the conditions associated with them. A recent estimate calculates that more than 4,000,000 bales of cotton were eliminated from this year's crop, adding about a quarter of a billion dollars to the growers' income for the season over what it would have been if the cotton plan had not been placed in operation. An attempt will be made to cut wheat acreage by 15 per cent, taking approximately 9,600,000 acres out of production. A processing tax of 30 cents per bushel, with appropriate conversion factors to make it effective on all products processed from wheat, has been levied. Corn and hogs may be approached from a single angle, since much of the former comes to market on the legs of the latter. Consequently the government has set in motion the machinery for buying at market premiums more than 4,000,000 pigs which will be slaughtered and processed and distributed through relief agencies this winter.

First consignments are already reaching many communities across the country. Agreements affecting milk and dairy products, as well as help to producers of a variety of other products, such as fruits and vegetables, beans, potatoes, poultry and eggs, are being put into operation as rapidly as possible all over the country.

But results are not yet encouraging. The Government has been forced to offer "loans" of 10 cents per pound to cotton growers on this year's crop in an effort to influence the price and achieve further reductions in acreage for next year. Receipts of wheat are considerably lower than last year, but the price has not been greatly influenced. Stating that "wheat sold in Grand Forks Saturday (October 14, 1933) for 53 cents (a bushel) which means ruin to many of our people if the prices in other lines continue to advance," the Governor of North Dakota signed a proclamation prohibiting shipments of wheat from the State, and called upon Governors of other wheat-producing States to coöperate with him. By arranging for the purchase of about a million bushels of wheat through the agencies of the Farm Credit Administration to be used by the Federal Emergency Relief Administration, the Government seeks to correct some of the disparities that have arisen.

AGRICULTURAL CREDIT

Title II of the Farm Relief Act seeks to meet the second of the two major problems harassing the farmer, that of his burden of indebtedness. During the Hoover administration a large number of public and semi-public agencies dealt with farm credit. Acting under his power to make changes in government executive and administrative agencies, President Roosevelt abolished some of the existing agencies, merged and reorganized others, and by an order issued in March, 1933, combined all the credit agencies under the Farm Credit Administration. It is through this Administration, and the agencies created by the Farm Credit Act of 1933, that farm credits will be spread out until they reach the smallest farmer in the local communities of the nation.

Under Part 1 of Title II of the Farm Relief Act, amendments to the Farm Loan Act make it possible for the Federal Land Banks to issue farm-loan bonds up to an aggregate amount of $2,000,000,000 for the purpose of making new loans, or for purchasing mortgages or exchanging bonds for mortgages. The interest, at a rate not to exceed 4 per cent per annum, is to be guaranteed by the government. The Federal Land Banks are authorized to engage in the purchase, reduction, and refinancing of farm mortgages within a limit of 50 per cent of the normal value of the land mortgaged and 20 per cent of the value of permanent insured improvements thereon.

To encourage the Federal Land Banks to extend obligations due them from farmers, the Secretary of the Treasury is authorized to subscribe to the paid-in surplus of such banks in amounts equal to the amount of the extensions and deferments made by the banks. By another amendment, interest rates on mortgage loans made by Federal Land Banks in certain cases are

limited to 4½ per cent, with a further provision that
if the borrower has not otherwise defaulted, payments
on the principal shall not be required for a period of
five years. In cases where losses may be sustained by
the Federal Land Banks on account of reductions in
interest, reimbursement is provided through payments
to be made by the Secretary of the Treasury out of an
appropriation of fifteen millions of dollars for that
purpose.

Where there are no national farm-loan associations
existing or effective, through which farmers may secure
loans, provisions are made for direct loans to farmers
through the Federal Land Banks under the authority
of the Farm Loan Commissioner. This is done under
an arrangement very much like the stock subscriptions
made by borrowers in the usual building and loan associations. Covenants in the mortgage look forward to
the formation of these borrowers, when there is a
sufficient number of them, into a national farm-loan
association; and the process is hastened by the promise
of reduced interest rates when such associations are
chartered.

Part 2 of this Title operates to liquidate Joint Stock
Land Banks. The RFC is authorized to loan money,
not to exceed 60 per cent of the normal value of the
real estate back of the loan, to these banks to assist
in their orderly liquidation, providing they reduce
interest rates to borrowers indebted to the bank to
5 per cent and agree not to proceed by foreclosure or
otherwise against the borrowers for a period of two
years. Further to prevent foreclosures, the Farm Loan

Commissioner is authorized to make emergency loans to these banks within certain limitations and subject to certain conditions.

Part 3 of the same Title makes available to the Farm Loan Commissioner through the agency of the RFC a fund of $200,000,000 for direct loans to farmers for the following purposes: (1) refinancing any indebtedness of the farmer, (2) providing working capital for his farm operations, (3) enabling him to redeem and/or repurchase farm property which was foreclosed at any time after July 1, 1931. A fund of $50,000,000 provided by the RFC under Part 4, is made available to help agricultural districts to refinance or reduce their indebtedness on improvement projects which, on appraisal, are found economically sound; while another section makes provision for the completion of similar projects now under construction through the operation of a reclamation fund under prior legislation.

The borrowing power of the RFC is enlarged to cover its obligations in connection with this Act. The Farm Loan Commissioner is brought within control of Executive Orders of the President; and the Governor of the Farm Credit Administration is authorized to perfect the Farm Credit Administration as he may deem necessary. There are other, minor, provisions respecting this part of farm credits which is given the short title "Emergency Farm Mortgage Act of 1933," but the principal ones have been stated. Title III of the Act deals wholly with questions of finance and will be treated under that head.

Of even greater significance in the field of farm

credits are the provisions made, and the organizations set up, under the Farm Credit Act of 1933 (Public No. 75, H.R. 5790) approved June 16, 1933. It is impossible in the present restricted space to discuss the Act in detail, but its major purposes and outlines may be indicated. Banking and credit institutions of four types are to be set up under the Act. They are: Production Credit Corporations (PCC), Production Credit Associations (PCA), Central Bank for Co-operatives, and regional Banks for Co-operatives. Twelve PCC, one in each city where a Federal Land Bank is located, are to be set up with an initial capital stock of $7,500,-000 to be subscribed by the Governor of the Farm Credit Administration on behalf of the United States. A revolving fund of $120,000,000, made up from contributions coming in part from the Treasury and in part from the RFC, is to be used for this purpose.

These Corporations are authorized to purchase Class A stock in PCA units formed within their respective districts to an amount approximately equal to 20 per cent of the volume of loans of such associations, but the amount may be increased by action of the Governor. The stock so purchased must be preferred as to assets on liquidation, entitled to dividends without discrimination, and shall not at any time exceed 75 per cent of the total paid-in capital of an association. Provisions are made for expenses, for the restoration of losses and impairments of capital, and for the creation of a surplus, after which any profits are to be invested in United States bonds, in Class A stocks of the PCA, or returned to the revolving fund for retirement of the stock of the PCC.

Production Credit Associations, under the complete supervision, control, and along the lines determined by the Governor of the FCA, may be formed by ten or more farmers wishing to borrow money under the Act. Two classes of stock, each of the par value of $5 per share, enter into the capital structure of these associations. Class A stock is to be taken by the PCC as above indicated. Class B stock, which alone has voting rights limited to one vote for each stockholder regardless of the amount of his holdings, will be held by those borrowing from the associations. Conversion over from B to A shares must be made within two years after loans have been repaid. Investors generally may hold Class A shares. Dividends limited to a maximum of 7 per cent may be declared, providing deficits have been made up, reserves for bad debts established, and a guarantee fund created, equal at least to 25 per cent of the association's paid-in capital. Subject to regulations prescribed by the PCC, loans, not less than $50 nor more than 20 per cent of the capital and guarantee fund of the association, may be made to borrowers who must own Class B stock amounting at least to 5 per cent of the size of the loan. Under certain circumstances, loans up to 50 per cent of the capital and guaranty fund of the association may be made. PCA units may borrow from and rediscount eligible paper with the Federal Intermediate Credit Banks, but with no other banking institution unless authorized by the Governor of the FCA.

Titles III and IV deal with the banks for coöperatives. The Governor of the FCA is to organize a corporation known as the Central Bank for Co-operatives. Its principal office is to be in the District of Columbia. The Co-operative Bank Commissioner of the FCA is to be one of seven directors three of whom ultimately will be selected by the borrowers, and all of whom are subject to removal by the Governor for cause. The Governor is to fix the amount of the capital stock, in shares of $100 par value, according to the needs of the borrowers who are to be coöperative associations and the Banks for Co-operatives. Out of the revolving fund made available to the Governor, he is to subscribe for stock in the Central Bank on behalf of the United States. Funds for operations will be derived from issues of debentures to an amount not exceeding five times the paid-in capital and surplus, secured by collateral of cash, direct obligations of the United States Government, and discounted or purchased notes, equal in amount at least to the debentures outstanding. Loans are to be made to coöperatives which, at the time of borrowing, are required to own $100 of stock for each $2,000 or fraction thereof of the amount borrowed. The stock, less impairments, is to be retired and paid off when the loan is repaid. For such coöperative associations as are unable to take stock by reason of restrictions under State laws, provision to achieve the same object through a guaranty fund is made. Subject to provisions against losses, impairments of capital and guaranty funds, and to insure a 25 per cent surplus, earnings to the maximum dividend of 7 per cent are to be shared by the stockholders and the depositors in the guaranty fund.

In each city where there is a Federal Land Bank, there is to be created by the Governor of the FCA a Bank for Co-operatives in which subscriptions for stock (including the Governor's subscription on behalf of the United States out of the revolving fund), earnings, reserves, and provisions for the distribution of profits, are determined along practically the same lines as for the Central Bank. Likewise, the Governor fixes the capital stock at a figure approximating the needs of the borrowers. Loans are to be made to coöperative associations for purposes set forth in the Agricultural Marketing Act.

On the surface it appears that this class of banks may overlap or otherwise interfere with the operations of the Central Bank since each is empowered to loan to coöperatives. In practice this is not likely to occur because of the fact that the Governor may circumscribe the field of each through a power to determine classes of borrowers and the amount of loans or both. It is not inconceivable that the Central Bank may come to occupy such a position with regard to the regional Banks for Co-operatives as does the Federal Reserve Board to the Federal Reserve Banks.

This Credit Act, together with the Agricultural Adjustment Act, constitutes the major foundations of the agricultural section of the Recovery Program. When the broad effect of the whole is fully grasped, the revelation is amazing. Without taking over agriculture, as was done in Russia, the Government has so penetrated the institutions and procedures of the industry, from the highest national groupings to the smallest local units throughout the land, as to gather into its hands absolute control over every act of production, processing, manufacturing, and marketing of practically all agricultural and associated commodities. Within the framework of the land bank system, it has established a net-work of banks and credit institutions adequate to meet almost every conceivable need for agricultural finance and credit. If developed and not upset, this alone may come to mean the end of the private financing of agricultural operations and the abolition of speculation purely for profit in agricultural products. The program affirms the determination of the Administration to organize agriculture from the soil to the market, which is a first essential step toward gearing agricultural productivity to effective consumptive capacity within the nation. The world has been waiting in vain since 1873 for one of the Western nations to realize the inevitability of such a step. From it, in time, true surpluses, such as Adam Smith envisaged in an international exchange of commodities, may emerge.

This is not to say that any task now attempted in agriculture is finished. The entire program in this field has merely entered upon a transition stage in which the major problems are still to be solved. The structure, erected with such haste and under such trying conditions over the past seven months, is very awkward, grotesque, and cluttered with useless débris. But from all appearances the lines of advance seem to point in the right direction—which is to overcome, in terms of the 20th century, the curious and mystifying paradox of want within the very presence of abundant supply.

CHAPTER VI

FINANCE

SECURITIES

SINCE 1900 the relationship between persons and tangible property has been altered rapidly and radically. The process had been going on for a long time but the acceleration over the last thirty years has been enormous. Even as late as the turn of the century, if a reputedly rich man was asked to describe his "wealth" he would, in all likelihood, detail the land, or the factory, or the ships, or the shop, or the bank, or even perhaps the gold, the silver, the diamonds, he owned. With but few minor exceptions, that was his conception of wealth. It supplied his needs and met his desires for material things, and around it he built his life and work. Should the same question be asked of the rich man of to-day, he is far more likely to exhibit his "portfolio" of stocks, bonds, notes, mortgages, and a miscellaneous collection of pieces of paper, all of which we group under the broad term, "securities." These are often described as "claims to wealth" which are realized principally through the medium of money income with which modern needs and desires for material things are satisfied. The differences so obvious in the illustration constitute one of the principal changes in the relationship between persons and tangible property. And rules that apply to man's property apply also to woman's.

The other major change, not so obvious from this illustration, is the new situation surrounding the ownership and control of tangible properties. In the days when a man owned a ship or a factory, ownership was an individual rite, uniting in the person of a single individual both the possession and absolute control of the physical, tangible property. This was true even under the device of co-partnerships; property possession still remained in the hands of individuals. But gradually with the coming of the corporation, and rapidly with the extension of the corporate idea over the last thirty years, individual persons were separated from the possession and control over tangible properties. Minor exceptions aside, a man no longer owned a ship or a factory; he owned a piece of paper which in law entitled him to participate, along with hundreds of other persons owning like slips of paper, in a corporation that owned the ship or the factory and controlled the properties for all practical, operating purposes. Ownership had become a collective rite, in which millions of women shared as never before in the history of economy.

Interesting and far-reaching as are these great changes, it is not with them that this section of the Recovery Program deals, except that they constitute the background out of which a new situation has arisen, namely the conditions and abuses which have accompanied the enormous issues and sales of securities. Of the total "wealth" attributed to the nation, almost 65

per cent consists or is described in terms of securities:
stocks and bonds of private corporations, of governments, federal, state, municipal and foreign, mortgages, and so on. The number of security holders has
grown to immense proportions and is diffused throughout the length and breadth of the land. An enormous
number of people have come to depend for their life
and work upon the income derived from the possession
and sale of securities. In the last ten years over sixty-
three billions of dollars of securities have been sold to
investors.

In the good old-fashioned horse trade (not necessarily the buying and selling of horses, but of any
tangible properties) people could know the conditions
of the bargain they were making and what they were
going to get because they were dealing in physical
objects. They could bring all their senses to bear upon
the transaction in the effort to arrive at an independent
judgment. If buyers and sellers sustained losses in
such transactions, the losses may be said to have been
legitimate, arising let us say from some want of skill
in calculation or judgment; they were less likely to be
losses arising from a total absence of knowledge of and
about the properties being bought and sold.

With securities forming the corpus of buying and
selling operations, the human senses are deprived of
the opportunity to reach an independent judgment. An
offer to sell "Exonerated Common" at $105 per share
conveys nothing to the buyer about what he is buying,
the properties behind the share of stock, the individuals who are controlling them, the soundness or

utility of the enterprise, and so on. The transaction takes on many features of the lottery or the gamble in which a rabbit's foot may be the best basis of judgment, and sometimes the only one. As was to be expected under such circumstances, cheating, deceit, corruption —some of it well within the law and the rules of the game, but immoral nevertheless—ran rampant in the field of corporate finance. The buyer was set upon by all the tricks of the trade—watered stock, sales to insiders on inside information, a maze of inter-company transactions, "pegged" markets, suppression of essential facts, a complexity of legal priorities skillfully phrased to sell the public something and give it nothing; the list is endless. The Securities Act of 1933 (Public No. 22, H.R.5480) approved May 27, 1933, was designed to cope with that situation.

Space prohibits a detailed analysis of the Act but its broad lines indicate how it is intended to operate. Federal, state, and municipal securities are exempted from the Act, as are those of government corporations, national and state supervised and controlled banks, Federal Reserve banks, commercial paper of limited operation, of corporations "not for pecuniary profit," of certain "mutual" institutions such as building and loan associations and the like, of common carriers subject to the Interstate Commerce Act, of receivers and trustees in bankruptcy, and certain classes of insurance policies and contracts. Small corporations may also be exempted under certain conditions. In addition, a number of specific transactions are also exempted from the operation of the Act.

All use of the mails and of other instruments of interstate commerce in connection with security issues or
sales is unlawful unless the security is registered. Almost two-thirds of the Act is then devoted to provisions
for the registration of securities. Registration must be
with the Federal Trade Commission. The purpose of
the registration statement is to provide for complete
and accurate information about the securities being
offered and sold. Some of the principal items are: detailed information about the names, addresses, and functions of the persons connected with the "issuer" of the
security, which includes all directors and officers of the
corporation, underwriters of the stock or bonds, persons owning more than 10 per cent of the stock of the
issuer and the amount of securities of the issuer each
such person holds or subscribes for; full disclosure of
the capital structure of the issuer; the funded debt outstanding; the amount, purpose, and characteristics of
the security being issued; salaries paid by the issuer to
its directors and officers; prices at which the securities
are to be offered to the public; commissions paid re-
gardless of in what form; provisions respecting properties acquired with the proceeds of securities issued;
details as to material contracts of a certain class; balance sheets and profit and loss statements of the issuer
and of any enterprise which the issuer may acquire
with the proceeds or through the securities issued;
copies of agreements with underwriters and with others
which may bear upon the securities issued; copies of
articles of incorporation and certain other classes of
corporate instruments. Similar detail, but adapted to

the different situation, is required for all issues of foreign securities. Provisions for making public the essential parts of these requirements are designed to assure protection for the security buyer and holder.

Remedies against any untrue statement of a material fact or the omission of such a fact are available to the public through provisions for suit against the persons who signed the registration statement, directors of the issuer, and a number of other persons connected with the issue of the securities. Criminal proceedings, involving a fine of $5,000 or five years imprisonment or both, may also be instituted for violations under the Act. Enforcement agencies include the Federal Trade Commission, regular officers of the Department of Justice, and the courts. Elaborate protection is afforded to cover cases where the violations are not deliberate or result from justifiable conditions, or from human failings in judgment.

Under Title II of the Act provision is made for the creation of a "Corporation of Foreign Security Holders" for the purpose of protecting, conserving, and advancing the interests of holders of foreign securities in default. Although linked with governmental supervision, the Corporation is not strictly a government agency, and the Act makes distinct provision against the assumption by the Corporation of any government sanctions.

Admittedly this is a sketchy outline of the Act, intended to give no more than a broad conception of the purpose sought to be achieved and the means provided. A storm of protest against the Act, none the less effectual because it is confined to small circles, has already arisen and may be counted upon to be aggressively operative in the next session of Congress. It has been said that the Act not only operates to prevent the issue of bad securities, but makes impossible the issue of any and all securities, hamstringing business and finance and delaying recovery. In each such criticism it is frankly admitted that investors need protection, and the purpose and intent of the Act is generously applauded. According to the critics of the Act, it is the detailed requirements, the administration and the manner by which these good intentions are to be realized, which constitute the real objections. All of which illustrates how extremely difficult it is to describe "honesty" in legal terms; how hard it is to narrow down the means by which in the past relatively few people have been able to prey upon the great majority of their fellows, and escape the responsibilities for their acts; what a task it is to prevent "operations" disclosed in such exposures as the Pujo investigation and the recent Senate inquiries on foreign bonds and stock market practices; and what a thankless undertaking it is to attempt to save some persons from enforced exile and disgrace, others from jail and suicide, and even many upright men from the consequences of their own shortcomings. Granted the Act has "rough" spots, granted it will never operate with complete justice, efficiency and dispatch, nevertheless, a disinterested appraisal of it cannot fail to sustain the conclusion that it will make less possible the abuses so flagrant and so tragic in the past.

Already subtle propaganda, some of it thinly veiled beneath the seemingly conscientious objections, is at work to undermine the Act, presumably for the benefit of the next Congress, where attempts will be made to render the Act more "workable" and "less obstructive to recovery," which in the majority of cases will come to mean whittling down the protection to the public into the thinness of that irresponsibility "on technical grounds," which has destroyed honesty and sincerity and morality in other days. Attempts to modify the Act ought to be watched with great care by the public, and no less by business and finance themselves, lest a law which may prevent fraud and deception, inflated stocks, insiders, bonus and pension and unconscionably high salary payments, rigged markets, fake bond and stockholders "protective" committees, "split-ups," and sometimes just plain "legal gambling," may be reduced to a pious aspiration.

THE BANKING ACT OF 1933

During the period 1921-1932 almost 9,000 State and private banks and more than 1,500 national banks suspended operations. Deposits involved in the former aggregated more than three and three-quarters billions of dollars, and in the latter close to one and one-quarter billions. It has not been merely since 1929 that these distressing suspensions have occurred; there has been a steady stream of them over the last ten years, even while "prosperity" waved the magic wand. No description is adequate to depict the losses of life savings, the maladjustments of businesses, the personal hardships and tragedies, the destruction of confidence with its menace to the nation, which follows in the wake of closed banks. Attempts have been made in the past to immunize society from the effects of such fatalities. The Federal Reserve Act was such an attempt, and notwithstanding its imperfections it was a long stride forward. The Banking Act of 1933 is another such step. It aims to correct certain abuses of banking principles and operations, to strengthen and broaden the Federal Reserve System, and to provide for the safety of deposits through the device of an insurance corporation.

The provisions of the Act may be grouped broadly into four sections: (1) strengthen and broaden the Federal Reserve System; (2) safeguarding the integrity of banking principles and operations; (3) greater control over banks; and (4) providing deposit insurance. None of these divisions, which are here merely arbitrary for presentation, is wholly exclusive; there are many points of contact among them all.

1. One of the strongest inducements likely to bring many non-member banks into the Federal Reserve System is, of course, the provisions for deposit insurance, but since the subject is one quite complete in itself, it will be treated under that heading. Through the permission now accorded to Reserve member banks to establish State-wide branches within any State which gives similar permission to its own banks, it is hoped to induce many large State banks to join the system. At least this seems to be the real intent of the enabling provision, rather than to project national banks into a

competition with State banks; because no branch can be established without the approval of the Comptroller of the Currency. Morris Plan banks, mutual savings banks and similar institutions are permitted to join the Reserve system in the same manner and subject to the same provisions of law as State banks and trust companies. Since these banks do not have capital in the sense used in connection with other types of banks, they may be eligible nevertheless if their surplus and undivided profits are as large as the capital required of a national bank in the same locality. Instead of subscribing for stock, they may make deposits pending changes in State laws for that purpose although there is a time limit on this privilege. All the restrictions and conditions on national banks or member banks operate as well upon new members wherever applicable.

2. The relations between banks and holding companies and affiliates are placed under strict supervision and broad control through the Federal Reserve Board and the Comptroller. In the case of security affiliates, the bank must divest itself of connections within a year, with penalties provided for violations. Holding companies controlling member banks are required to secure a permit from the Federal Reserve Board in order to vote the stock of the bank; and by the reports required, the examinations to be made, the provisions for the accumulation of reserves by the holding company, and other supervisory conditions, the abuses formerly growing out of these relationships, it is hoped, will be eliminated. Restrictions surround bank loans

to its affiliates. Affiliates are placed under certain liabilities on bank shares held by them. Detailed provisions are made to get banks out of the security
business, and security companies out of the banking
business; since these relationships were among the principal means by which bank financial structures had
been weakened during recent years.

3. The Federal Reserve Board is given broad powers
to check the amount of reserve credit which is likely
to find its way through bank loans into speculations in
securities, real estate, and commodities. Through the
creation of an agency, the "Federal Open Market
Committee," and the subjection of Reserve banks to
regulations of the Board, attempts will be made to control and coördinate open market operations; while the
time, character, and volume of all purchases and sales
of paper eligible for open market operations will be
regulated for the accommodation of commerce and
business and with regard to the credit situation
throughout the country. These provisions may go a
long way toward achieving greater stability of business
conditions in the future.

A wider and more detailed control over the operations of banks and bank officials is provided for in a
number of places throughout the Act. Minimum limits
as to capitalization are placed upon national banking
associations which establish branches. The right of
banks to act as agents of non-banking institutions in
making loans on securities is prohibited. Member
banks are prohibited from paying interest on demand
deposits, and the Federal Reserve Board is given con-

trol over the rate of interest paid by member banks on time deposits. Greater responsibility is required of directors: their number shall not be less than five nor more than twenty-five; each director must be a bona fide owner of not less than $1,000 of stock in the bank; they are to be removed from office under certain conditions; and cumulative voting provisions in the election of directors assure representation to minority stockholders. No officer or director may be connected with a security company; and no member bank may perform the functions of a correspondent bank on behalf of security companies or anyone connected with them; while the latter may not perform the functions of a correspondent for any member bank, except by permit of the Reserve Board in special cases which are not incompatible with the public interest. Member bank loans to its officers are prohibited under penalty.

The Federal Reserve Board is given supervision over all relationships and transactions of any kind between any Federal Reserve bank and any foreign bank or banker. Permission from the Board is required before officers or representatives of Reserve banks may conduct negotiations with foreign banks or bankers. The Board may also prescribe regulations bearing upon such matters, may be entitled to be represented, and shall be given a full report of all conferences, negotiations, understandings and agreements resulting.

4. A considerable portion of the Act is devoted to the arrangements regarding deposit insurance. A "Federal Deposit Insurance Corporation" is created "whose duty it shall be to purchase, hold, and liquidate

. . . the assets of national banks which have been closed by action of the Comptroller of the Currency, or by vote of their directors, and the assets of State member banks which have been closed by action of the appropriate State authorities, or by vote of their directors; and to insure . . . the deposits of all banks which are entitled to the benefits of insurance under this section."

A board of three directors, consisting of the Comptroller of the Currency and two citizens of the United States to be appointed by the President by and with the advice and consent of the Senate, is to manage the Corporation. The Corporation is vested with practically all of the usual corporate powers, and the directors are to prescribe by laws for the general conduct of its business. The Corporation is given certain government privileges and under certain conditions may avail itself of the information, service, and facilities of government agencies.

The capital is drawn from three sources: (1) $150,-000,000 from the Treasury through the subscription of the Secretary on behalf of the United States; (2) approximately $135,000,000 which is to come from the requirement that every Federal Reserve bank shall subscribe to Class B stock to an amount equal to one-half its surplus on January 1, 1933 (half to be paid in and half to be subject to call on 90 days' notice); (3) approximately (though flexible) $200,000,000 from banks participating in the permanent scheme through subscriptions of one-half of one per cent of their total deposit liabilities; so that at the outset the Corporation will have on hand and on call a total of half a billion dollars.

Class B stock is to be held only by the Federal Reserve banks, and is not to receive dividends. Class A stock is to be held by member and non-member banks which are to receive dividends out of net earnings at 6 per cent, cumulative, or to the extent of 30 per cent of net earnings in any one year, whichever is greater. Class A stock has no vote at stockholders' meetings. Class A stock holdings are to be adjusted annually on the basis of deposits. Banks which are or become members of the Reserve system on or before July 1, 1934, are required to take all steps to enable themselves to become Class A stockholders of the Corporation by that date. Certification on the basis of examinations provided for is to be made concerning the adequacy of the assets of the banks to meet the liabilities of their depositors and creditors. The benefits of this section of the Act are to be extended upon certain conditions to any State bank or trust company or mutual savings bank which applies for Federal Reserve membership or conversion into a national banking association on or before July 1, 1936. In cases where State banks, trust companies or mutual savings banks are unable, because of prohibiting State laws, to purchase stock in the Corporation, they may secure the benefits of the Act temporarily through a deposit arrangement; but unless enabling acts are passed by the State legislatures concerned, they may be compelled to withdraw from participation in the Corporation.

Beginning July 1, 1934, unless the President by

proclamation shall fix an earlier date, the Corporation shall insure the deposits of all member banks, and on and after such date until July 1, 1936, of all non-member banks which are Class A stockholders of the Corporation. Deposits are to be insured in the following amounts: 100 per cent up to $10,000; 75 per cent of any amount exceeding $10,000 but not exceeding $50,000; and 50 per cent of net amounts exceeding $50,000. The limitations on the coverage of large deposits are expected to insure watchfulness over the bank's operations by the larger depositors. Under these provisions more than 90 per cent of all depositors will be fully covered.

Upon the closing of a participating national bank, the Corporation becomes its receiver. It immediately forms a new national bank to assume the insured deposit liabilities of the closed bank; and makes available to the new bank an amount sufficient to cover the insured deposits which are then at the disposal of depositors. This is an ingenious device which relieves the strain on the insurance fund by exploiting that psychology by which depositors are likely to leave the greater portion of their insured deposits in the new bank subject only to current needs. The idea is further strengthened by the provision that the new bank may receive new deposits, and eventually bring itself into the position of a sound and regular bank, whereupon it may be authorized to commence a regular banking business. If this should not work out however, the Corporation may dispose of the new bank by transfer or liquidation. The Corporation endeavors to realize upon the assets of the closed bank, enforces the individual liability of the stockholders and directors, and may proceed to wind up its affairs.

Similar procedure, with the exception that it is adapted to the different conditions, is provided for the handling of State member banks upon their becoming insolvent, while participating in the benefit of the deposit insurance. Except for designated depositories for funds, the moneys of the Corporation are to be invested in securities of the United States Government. The Corporation is empowered to issue and have outstanding at any one time securities in an amount aggregating not more than three times the amount of its capital. Except for its real estate, the Corporation and all its securities are exempt from taxation. An annual report to Congress is required.

A temporary insurance plan is to go into effect on January 1, 1934, and is to be operative until July 1, 1934. A Temporary Federal Deposit Insurance Fund, substantiated by assessments of one-half of one per cent of the certified deposits of all participating banks, is to be set up. Provision is made for one additional assessment in the same amount from each member of the Fund if the Corporation requires it. Member banks are required to become members of the Fund, and sound non-member banks are permitted to join. Banks closed during the operation of the Fund are to be handled in a manner similar to that provided for operations under the permanent insurance plan. Deposits under the temporary plan are insured only to the extent of $2,500. The balance remaining in the

Fund on July 1, 1934, is to be refunded to all solvent participants.

A provision which seems to look forward to the relief of depositors in closed banks is as follows: "Receivers or liquidators of member banks which are now or may hereafter become insolvent or suspended shall be entitled to offer the assets of such banks for sale to the Corporation or as security for loans from the Corporation. . . ." Undoubtedly it was the intention when this provision was written into the law to make the Corporation a broad liquidating agency not only for the fiscal operations of the future through deposit insurance but also to "thaw" deposits in banks already closed. These banks were a hang-over from the crisis and before, and it is fair to say that the Government never lost sight of the serious problem they raised. In the attention paid to other purposes of larger scope in the banking Act under discussion, the above provision seems not to have attracted serious attention, and to date seems to have atrophied while steps have been taken through other agencies to liquidify the assets of closed banks.

There are still other ends sought to be achieved by the 1933 banking Act, such as for example that contemplated through the provision for short-term advances to member banks from the Reserve banks, but it is believed that the principal parts of the Act have been covered. What of the results? From latest information it seems certain that the temporary deposit insurance will go into effect on January 1, 1934, as planned. The Treasury is reported (New York *Times*,

October 19, 1933) to be busy compiling lists of banks which will be open when the guarantee practice goes into effect. Practically all banks which have reopened since the crisis will be included. Through the RFC banking capital is being substantiated to enable all banks with reasonably sound assets to qualify themselves for participation in the deposit insurance. Banks themselves have been busy on a campaign to clean up all slow or otherwise undesirable accounts so as to place themselves in a more favorable condition in the light of deposit insurance requirements. This latter effort, however, has led to hardships for those against whom the bank policy of cleaning up has operated; and it is to be hoped that the campaign will not be pushed too hard between now and January 1, or between that date and July 1, 1934, when the permanent deposit insurance plan goes into effect. It cannot be expected however, to escape some clearing-up operations, since it was largely the accumulations of obligations of this type that had weakened the financial structure before the crisis.

While the progress in broadening the Federal Reserve System through the admission of non-member banks has not definitely been reported upon, the statement of the condition of bank members of the system reveals the fact that the system is nearing the close of a transition position during which many loose ends have been gathered in, that much cleaning up has been done, and the whole system is placed in a condition for greater flexibility and stronger participation in whatever developments are to come over the next six months. Thus while loans outstanding have decreased over those of a year ago on October 19, bank reserves have increased, as have government deposits, cash in vaults, and net demand deposits.

There are approximately 8,600 State banks outside the Reserve system. With the system itself in something of a "ready" position, government efforts seem to have shifted toward improving the condition of these non-member banks. This is to be done mainly through the device of having the RFC purchase preferred stock or capital notes to be issued by these banks with the expected result of strengthening their capital structure and qualifying them for participation in the deposit insurance plan. Some 2,171 of these banks have already applied for membership in the Insurance Corporation, and it is reported that additional applications are coming in at the rate of 200 a day. A large field force is engaged in examining the condition of the banks seeking admission, in an effort to certify their qualifications as quickly as possible.

Meanwhile, through the efforts of a new agency— the Deposit Liquidation Board—created as a division of the RFC, an early attempt will be made to free at least one billion dollars of the deposits which have been frozen in the banks which have never opened since the crisis last winter.

Credit operations along many lines have already been shown in connection with enterprise under the Recovery Program. It should not be overlooked that the great credit reservoir is the Reconstruction Finance Corporation (RFC). This agency, created by Con-

gress in January, 1932, is woven into and is at the base
of every part of the Recovery Program. Originally
launched with a Government capital of $500,000,000
and power to issue bonds to a total of a billion and a
half dollars, its capital resources have been enlarged
by additional legislation which directed that its borrowing capacity was to be increased by such amounts as
may be necessary to enable it to carry out the particular added functions. Since its operations began, a
total of close to three billions of dollars in loans has
been extended. In the beginning its operations were
confined to aiding banks, railroad companies, insurance
companies, and various governmental divisions and
semi-public agencies, principally. Since that time, its
functions have been broadened to take in the whole
sweep of the Recovery Program. It is now supplying
credit to agriculture, industry, to home and other mortgage debtors, and for distress relief in many directions.
To the RFC policy of the former administration of
aid from the top down, the new administration has
added the policy of relief from the bottom up; and
now for the first time a balanced system is beginning
to operate.

INFLATION AND THE GOLD POLICY

Before talking about inflation one should first define
it. To define it intelligently it would be necessary to
discuss in detail every variety of action which might
possibly be construed to constitute somebody's idea of
inflation. The result would be a deluge of presump-
tions, suppositions, probabilities, conjectures, and

prophecies beneath which the reader would be sunk. In this instance the lack of space is a life saver all around. There is in legal pleading a device known as a "demurrer" which, broadly, admits all the facts of a case, and then in the language of the street says, "So what?" Such a device might well be the guide here. What are the Government's principal powers over the currency system, what is it doing with them, and what might be said about it?

The principal "inflationary" powers came first from the Agricultural Adjustment Act, part of which has already been discussed in another connection. The Act indicates some of the purposes for which the President's powers have been granted. They are: (1) to offset the effects upon American foreign commerce of depreciated foreign currencies; (2) to regulate and maintain the parity of currency issues of the United States; (3) to meet an economic emergency by an expansion of credit; and (4) to bring about an expansion of credit if an international stabilization agreement should require it. To attain any of these ends, the President is authorized, in his discretion—

1. To utilize the Federal Reserve System (so far as that is possible through agreements between the Secretary of the Treasury and the Reserve Board and Reserve Banks) (a) to conduct open market operations in obligations of the United States Government or corporations in which the United States is a majority stockholder, and (b) to purchase directly and hold in portfolio for agreed periods of time Treasury bills or other obligations of the United States Government in an aggregate sum of $3,000,000,000.

2. If the above device cannot be effected, or if it does

not prove satisfactory, or for any other reason, the President may direct the Secretary of the Treasury to issue United States notes in the usual denominations for the purpose of meeting maturing Federal obligations, to repay sums borrowed by the United States, and for purchasing United States bonds and other interest-bearing obligations of the United States—not to exceed an aggregate amount outstanding at any one time of $3,000,000,000. Such notes are to be legal tender for all debts public and private.

3. To vary, by proclamation, the weight of the gold dollar; but not to reduce it by more than 50 per cent of its (then) present weight. To fix the weight of the silver dollar at a definite fixed ratio to the gold dollar.

4. To accept silver from foreign debtors up to an amount of $200,000,000 at a price not to exceed 50 cents an ounce in United States currency. To issue silver certificates against this silver and use them in payment of any obligations of the United States. To reissue and keep such certificates in circulation, and to coin such portions of the metal as may be required for redemption purposes.

5. The Federal Reserve Board, by vote of five of its members and with the approval of the President, is given the power to increase or decrease from time to time in its discretion the reserve balances required to be maintained against either demand or time deposits.

Here are enormous powers which, it may be presumed, almost anyone versed with finance will describe as inflationary. Other considerations must be added. The country is definitely "off the gold standard," so that conversion of currency into gold is impossible. But more than that, through the President's direction to the RFC, the Government is to buy newly mined gold at prices above the world market. A recent step in relation to gold is the announced intention to buy and sell gold in the world market. It should be frankly stated that the Administration seeks to prevent any gold within the country from finding its way abroad; but more than that, it seeks to drain all the gold within the country into the Government hopper and there subject it to Government possession and control. Why?

The President has given a number of reasons, all more or less inter-related. He seeks "to restore commodity price levels, . . . to make possible the payment of public and private debts more nearly at the price level at which they were incurred, . . . to restore a balance in the price structure so that farmers may exchange their products for the products of industry on a fairer exchange basis, . . . to prevent prices from rising beyond the point necessary to attain these ends." After having restored the price level, an attempt will be made "to establish and maintain a dollar which will not change its purchasing and debt-paying power during the succeeding generation." Recognizing that there is an international aspect to domestic price levels and monetary policies, the President declared: "Our dollar is now altogether too greatly influenced by the accidents of international trade, by the internal policies of other nations, and by political disturbances in other continents."

"Therefore the United States must take firmly in its own hands the control of the gold value of our dollar. This is necessary in order to prevent dollar disturbances from swinging us away from our ultimate goal, namely, the continued recovery of our commodity prices. . . . My aim in taking this step [establishing a government market for gold in the United States and buying and selling gold in the world market] is to establish and maintain continuous control. This is a policy and not an expedient. . . . We are thus continuing to move toward a managed currency."

Here then, are two situations: the existence of so-called "inflationary" powers, and a gold policy. The country fears that something "radical" will be done about the former and the world is mystified about what is being done under the latter. For the moment conjectures are useless.

What of the "open market operations" through the Federal Reserve System? Beginning with the last week in August, the Reserve banks increased their purchases and holdings of government securities from ten millions of dollars per week to a rate of 35 millions of dollars. Throughout September and October they maintained the higher rate. On August 19, their holdings totaled 2,059 millions of dollars, and by October 21, this figure had risen to 2,375 millions of dollars, or an increase over the period of $316,000,000. Activities in bills seem to be at a low ebb.

What of money in circulation? Printing press money would be bound to show itself in this item. The daily average of money in circulation on October 21, 1933, was 5,665 millions of dollars as against 6,998 millions for the month of March average, and 5,641 millions on October 22, 1932. Certainly there is here no such increase as was contemplated by the power to issue United States notes up to three billions of dollars. There has been no announcement reducing the weight of the gold dollar; nor has there been any announcement of change in the reserve balances required to be maintained against either demand or time deposits. In the field of the Government's gold operations no appreciable change in either domestic prices or the state of the dollar abroad occurred in the closing week of October, during which the monetary policy may be said to have been active. However, at this writing no final word can be said, since time has merely commenced on the gold policy. The only result in this field seems to have been the apprehension of foreign countries over the possibility of a monetary war involving the dollar, pound, and franc, with President Roosevelt being reported as having no such intention.

We are still in the realm of fact on inflation. Are there any other developments? The October 30, 1933, Treasury Statement reports the public debt to be $23,-051,396,621.77 as against $20,813,560,036.51 of a year ago, an increase of slightly over two and a quarter billions of dollars. The excess of expenditures over the total general fund receipts is $227,709,009.24. This is less than the excess on the corresponding period of last year if the items may be considered comparable, for although we have spent more during the month reported on, we have also taken in larger receipts. If a like comparison be made between the excess of expenditures over receipts for the fiscal years 1934 and 1933, the excess of expenditures in the former appears to be but less than half of the latter. One final consideration running through all these figures and operations (a fact which must never be lost sight of for one moment when discussing inflation) is that within the United States, currency is not convertible into gold (rather it is a crime to have gold), and that in the international field severe restrictions rest upon the exportation of gold from this country.

The foregoing appear to be the principal facts bearing upon inflation. To answer the question, is or will there be inflation, is beside the point so far as the past is concerned. The facts speak for themselves. But to predict the future, it would be necessary to bring in every theory touching upon inflation, whereupon the discussion would take on the character of an argument of probabilities, the maintenance of some particular theory of chance, a hope, a wish, or at best a prophecy depending more upon luck than anything else for its validity.

CHAPTER VII

RELIEF AND PUBLIC WORKS

MANY of the items already discussed in other sections of the Recovery Program have all the characteristics of what is commonly considered "relief". In a civilization of relatively high living standards, of a highly complex and yet extremely delicate economic organization, the conception of relief must and does take on a broader meaning than the mere prevention of starvation and destitution. Suffering may be none the less poignant and distress may be none the less menacing and destructive to the stability of the nation because they take place on higher levels than those of primitive society. Whether so conceived or not, the Recovery Program has embraced this wider meaning of relief and seems to have demonstrated it well in the fields of industry and transportation, finance, and agriculture. There remains a number of items more closely associated with the narrower conception of relief, although even these matters assume a wider aspect than that of providing essential subsistence and of alleviating physical suffering from other causes. For convenience these items are grouped in two broad categories: distress relief and public works. Neither is exclusive of the other and both are bound up with a broad characterization of the whole Recovery Program.

In his statement issued at the signing of the National Industrial Recovery Act, the President declared: "In my inaugural I laid down the simple proposition that nobody is going to starve in this country." Speaking before the Conference on Mobilization for Human Needs, held at Washington in September, 1933, the President stated that meeting the emergency of human needs was first of all a matter for the citizens of a community acting through the churches, the community chest, the social and charitable organizations of the community; and second, a matter for local government; and then if those agencies should prove inadequate, the next unit—the State—must be brought into play; and if that is still not enough, "then obviously the Federal Government must step in, because, while it isn't written in the Constitution, nevertheless it is the inherent duty of the Federal Government to keep its citizens from starvation." In creating the Federal Emergency Relief Administration, the President stated that he was striking at the paradox whereby the unemployed were allowed to go hungry while the farms were choked with an abundance of surplus products. The ultimate link in the chain of principles bearing upon distress relief seems to have been forged by the President, when in his radio speech on October 22, he declared: " . . . if there is any family in the United States about to lose its home or about to lose its chattels, that family should telegraph at once either to the Farm Credit Administration or the Home-Owners Loan Corporation in Washington requesting their help."

Here appear to be the simple outlines—the principles —of a highly significant step for America—the positive assurance that the people shall not want for at least the basic necessities of life. The significance does not lie so much in the actual provision of those necessities as it does in the assurance, almost amounting to a guarantee, that they shall have them as a matter of right. If in practice, relief operations are carried on within the spirit of such an assurance, and the psychology and stigma of charitable dispensation are thereby removed, relief activities will have laid the firm foundation for one of the greatest advances in practical humanity the world has ever seen. Beside such an achievement, all the other parts of the Recovery Program, whatever their significance, would be of secondary importance. For it would go down in history that in the twentieth century, one nation, profoundly stirred by the realization that abject poverty and destitution among its people was absolutely unnecessary, had resolved to abolish human starvation and insecurity from its land by rational action.

Under these principles, the Federal Emergency Relief Administration set in motion plans to purchase $75,000,000 worth of surplus food and clothing for distribution to the unemployed. More than 100,000,000 pounds of cured pork for similar distribution were brought under the program. The plans also include the purchase of approximately $30,000,000 worth of dairy products. Butter purchases at the rate of nine million pounds per month are aimed to relieve glutted markets from a surplus of more than seventy million pounds. A plan for buying beef—range cattle, particularly breeders—is aimed to reduce that surplus, raise the average price of beef cattle, and at the same time carry out the relief purposes of the administration. A wheat purchase of approximately 1,000,000 bushels has also been arranged for, with additional purchases, possibly as high as a total of forty million bushels, in contemplation for the winter. Most of these purchases are to be made through the newly created agency, the Surplus Relief Corporation, while actual distribution of the commodities is to be achieved through the Emergency Relief Administration working through the net-work of State and local relief agencies all over the country.

The success of these plans depends in the last analysis on the spirit and the efficiency with which they are carried out. If they are to be carried out as relief has been provided in the past—with endless red tape, with the subjection of the individual to the disgrace and ignominy of a third degree far more destructive than that of physical torture because it beats down self-respect and morality—they might better be withheld and the inexorable forces of nature permitted to operate unassisted by the cruelties of man to man. What is needed in connection with relief is some device by which the individual, having once established his willingness to work in the field in which his talents and training normally fit him or for which he may be reasonably prepared, and having established his inability to find such employment in some simple way which is not demeaning to his self-respect, may receive adequate relief for himself and his immediate family as a matter of right. This might easily be achieved through the proper organization and operation of the federal employment service which is elsewhere discussed.

Finally, that which is now regarded as an emergency function or institution must somehow be revised as to operate as a permanent institution until more wholesome processes of economic life are made workable. People cannot always be kept in the present high pitch of sympathy toward their stricken fellows. As re-employment spreads and the number of unfortunates dwindles, those remaining are quite likely to be forgotten, as was the plight of the farmers and the miners and many other groups during the period of high "prosperity" when the permanent unemployed totaled two million. Moreover all persons across the country are not yet imbued with the principles behind the present relief plans, nor are all people convinced that starvation and destitution should and can be eradicated. And many of these people will be operating relief machinery after the present dire emergency is past and under their narrow conceptions of economy relief may again sink back into the disgraceful thing it once was. This must be prevented at all events. It can be done only by building now, while the materials and the right conditions are at hand, permanent institutions so grounded in the economic and social life that they will carry their beneficence into the future upon their own momentum.

Other parts of the Recovery Program are designed to relieve distress. The Wagner-Lewis Emergency Relief Law, approved May 12, makes available from funds of the RFC $500,000,000 for this purpose and some of it has been used by the Federal Emergency Relief Administrator directly as above indicated. It is designed also to make grants to States in aid of their own relief work. The march of a "bonus army" upon Washington during the Hoover administration, and the discovery by the Senate that there were thousands of young men roaming about the country seeking work and living a precarious existence, prompted the passage of another law designed to meet that condition, while women were left to shift for themselves, in the main.

The Unemployment Relief Act (Public No. 5, S.598) approved in March, 1933, authorized the President to employ citizens in the construction, maintenance, and carrying on of works of a public nature in connection with the natural resources of the country. Under this law, the Citizens Civilian Conservation Corps was created and absorbed approximately 300,000 men, placing them in well-constructed camps throughout the country, and turning them to such work as the prevention of forest fires, floods and soil erosion, plant pest and disease control, the construction of paths, trails and fire lanes in the national parks and forests, and other activities on the public domain.

HOME OWNERS' RELIEF

On June 13, 1933, the President approved the "Home Owners' Loan Act of 1933" (Public No. 43, H.R.5240) which creates a Home Owners' Loan Corporation, with a capital of $200,000,000 to be subscribed by the Secretary of the Treasury on behalf of the United States from funds to be made available to him through the RFC. The Corporation is also authorized to issue bonds up to two billions of dollars, the interest upon which is to be guaranteed by the United States Government. Except for its real estate, the Corporation and its properties are to be exempt from taxation, as are also its bonds except as to surtaxes, inheritance, and gift taxes. The Corporation is authorized, for a period of three years, to exchange bonds for home mortgages and other obligations and liens secured by real estate, up to $14,000 in each case. Home owners are to amortize the mortgages or liens over a period of fifteen years. For similar purposes the Corporation may make loans upon property not otherwise encumbered up to 50 per cent of the value of the property. In cases where the home owner cannot be relieved through the operation of the provision for the exchange of bonds for mortgages, the Corporation may make loans not exceeding 40 per cent of the value of the property at a rate of interest not to exceed 6 per cent, and in that manner aid home owners to reduce the extent of their indebtedness to private lenders. By another provision, both cash and bonds are made available for the redemption of properties from foreclosure.

One of the most important provisions of the Act, aside from relief to home owners, is the authority vested in the Federal Home Loan Bank Board to provide for the organization and operation of "Federal Savings and Loan Associations" for the purpose of encouraging mutual thrift and home-financing institutions in the United States. The provisions for these institutions might be made to yield incalculable benefit to the people of this country, and it is disappointing at the moment to the sponsors of the Act that there is not greater activity upon the part of citizens of the country and the Government itself in the formation of these institutions.

Under the operations of the Act, it was reported on October 29, some 22,832 mortgages having a total value of $65,271,957 have been refinanced or otherwise handled with relief to home owners. Up to October 20, a total of 86,220 applications calling for $244,082,233 had been tentatively approved. The report of the Corporation recounts similar progress on other loan and relief provisions of the Act.

The Act should not be confused with the Home Loan Bank System which had been created as a permanent mortgage credit reserve system dealing with home-mortgage lending institutions and not with individual lenders and borrowers. The latter was created under the former administration and appears to be performing a useful function in its special sphere.

EMPLOYMENT SERVICE

Finally, in the forces working toward relief, there is the Act providing for the establishment of a national employment system. The Act creates a bureau known as the "United States Employment Service" within the Department of Labor. The bureau is "to promote and develop a national system of employment offices for men, women, and juniors who are legally qualified to engage in gainful occupations, to maintain a veterans' service . . . securing employment for veterans, to maintain a farm placement service. . . ." The bureau is to work in coöperation with the several States and assist in coördinating the public employment offices throughout the country. The sum of $1,500,000 is appropriated for the fiscal year ending 1934, and $4,000,000 for each fiscal year thereafter until June 30, 1938. Seventy-five per cent of the amounts appropriated is to be made available to the States on a population basis, providing each State appropriates a sum equal to the amount which may be apportioned to it. States availing themselves of the Act are required to submit plans for the approval of the Federal Director. The remaining portion of the appropriation, and in certain cases part of the apportioned funds, may be spent by the Federal Director in maintaining systems of employment offices in States where there are no public employment services or where no State appropriations have been made. Besides the Federal Director and the Federal bureau, and the coöperative action with the States, the Act provides for Federal and State Advisory Councils. The Act envisages vocational rehabilitation as well as interstate placements of workers.

One of the principal faults of the Act is the failure to broaden its scope by a direct mandate to survey the unemployed. Admirable as the Act is to correct the evils of private employment agencies it does not reach far enough. After four years of an economic depression, with constantly mounting figures of unemployment, we are still "estimating" the number of men out of work, and the estimates vary considerably according to the special interests of those offering the estimates. Unemployment on such a scale as we have had and still have is too serious a problem for "estimates." We should know. We should know the number of persons out of work, their age and sex classifications, their former occupations, their talents and capacities, the number of persons dependent upon them. We should know the geographical distribution of unemployment. In wartime, we did not "estimate" the number of men available for military service; we found out definitely. The exigency is just as great in this peace-time emergency; and while it may not be expedient to go so far as compulsory registration, many positive steps could be taken in that direction. If the country does take on a Fascist complexion, it will be done under far less pleasant circumstances and for a much less praiseworthy purpose. Transient employments might complicate the effort, but they would not vitiate a well-constructed plan. As additional positive benefits it is conceivable that such a plan might assist in the reduction of crime and in the prevention of relief frauds, while on the other hand it might play a vital part in rendering distress relief more efficient and more humane.

MEANS OF CONTACT

To detail all of the agencies at work in the prevention of starvation and destitution is a task for much more space than is here allotted, but the major outlines of the forces now at work have been indicated. Greater simplicity is needed in the contact between all these services and the people at large. The people do not seem to be half aware of the help ready at hand. They are confused and bewildered by the maze of agencies at work, and they do not know where to turn. Inertia and a feeling of futility are often the result; and these, however unjustified they may be, operate as a bar to the return of confidence, an obstruction to recovery, and may even be productive of more dire consequences.

This whole fabric of relief—distress relief, debt relief, unemployment relief, and all the rest of it—is in great need of some simple agency in every community which will perform for the people at large the kind of coördinating public-contact service which a mail order catalogue performs between millions of individual buyers and the great organization ready to fill their needs. True, the President indicated the need of such a simple procedure when he directed any home owner about to lose his home or his chattels to telegraph at once to Washington; but even the President must realize the inadequacy of that direction in the great majority of cases. The machinery at hand necessarily involves collective dealing with groups of persons, categories of things, organizational structures, but the cases are predominantly individual before they enter the collective machinery. There must be some simple point of contact between the two.

The principle here advanced is not novel. It is already in wide use. The receiving ward of a hospital is such an agency, and the general diagnostician of a private clinic performs a similar service. With business so complex, business and commercial firms have themselves applied the idea in their contacts with the people directly and through their advertisements. Department stores and many public buildings have an information service at a strategic point. Every office of any size has a general clerk who meets all comers, ascertains the nature of their wants, and arranges for the proper individual to care for them.

Government—Democracy itself—adopted the idea, when Congress, baffled by the avalanche of problems, the confusion of agencies and the inability to get things done or move in any direction, finally made of the Presidency a single, executive coördinating agency standing between the needs of the country and the machinery designed to supply them. It may well be that the action of the Congress in this respect saved Democracy as a political institution, for its very foundations were menaced by the seeming inability to take effective action.

The relief program as above laid out appears to be capable of meeting every reasonable demand, but it is suffering from the same disease as Congress was in March, 1933—the lack of a simple, direct, and executive contact between the individual needs of the people and the maze of agencies ready at hand to serve them. Is there any wonder that there are complaints and unrest and impatience with the Recovery Program? Many of them would have little standing if it could be positively shown that relief and assistance are available. There is no use in broadcasting in the press and otherwise that a mass of government agencies have been created to meet every legitimate call for help. Despite the spread of education, the rank and file are still strangers to government agencies; and it is necessary to point out one place for them to go to in their county or city, one individual to see and talk to, irrespective of what their problems may be. That single, contact agency or individual should be thoroughly versed with the government program and all the agencies created to carry it out, and should know how to place such information at the service of the people. Until that lack is supplied, genuine relief will be "spotty" and its forces will remain inefficient, spending their energies as in the past without ever realizing the great ideals they were set up to attain.

PUBLIC WORKS

There are two classes of public works embraced within the Recovery Program. There are first the usual government projects, such as the construction of post offices, other public buildings, bridges, roads, drainage projects, river and harbor works, naval construction, municipal and local projects, and the like. Second there are those projects which are to be permanent government enterprises. The two are quite distinct although they both serve a single present need. The latter, however, have a far-reaching significance for the economic structure of society in the future, and it is this which distinguishes them from the usual public works program.

The first category derives its major authority from

Title II of the National Industrial Recovery Act. Under it, the President was authorized to create a Federal Emergency Administration of Public Works to be under the direction of an Administrator who is granted broad powers. The Administrator is directed to prepare a comprehensive program of public works embracing the following major projects: (1) construction, repair and improvement of highways, parkways, public buildings, and the like; (2) conservation and development of natural resources; (3) any public projects heretofore carried on by public authorities in the interest of the general public; (4) low-cost housing and slum clearance projects; (5) other projects, including naval construction and army improvement.

To bring about immediate employment, the Act empowers the President to make outright grants to public bodies and other agencies up to 30 per cent of the cost of the labor and materials used. Some four hundred millions of dollars may be made available to States for highway purposes under the Federal Highway Act. Contracts are to contain provisions limiting hours of work to thirty per week, and require the payment of just and reasonable wages which shall be sufficient to provide, for the hours of labor as limited, "a standard of living in decency and comfort." To expedite work, advance loans may be made to contractors. The sum appropriated for the purposes of the Act is $3,300,-000,000 of which part, not to exceed one hundred million dollars may be allocated to the Farm Credit Administration for the purposes of the agricultural program.

The Act was approved by the President on June 16,
1933. The most recent report from the Federal Administrator's office states that total allotments to date are
$2,049,767,088, leaving approximately $1,250,000,000
still to be utilized. Of the total allocated, $1,802,116,-
926 is on Federal, and $247,650,162 on non-Federal,
or State and local projects. The disproportion between
the two is to be corrected by the plan to use the major
part of the unallotted balance for non-Federal projects.
It is possible also that the present disproportion is due,
in some measure, partly to Federal red tape and restrictions and partly to the difficulties encountered in assisting State, local and other agencies. Several of the
major allotments as reported by the Administrator are:
"Federal aid highway projects, $400,000,000; Civilian
Conservation Corps, $301,037,315; naval construction,
$238,000,000; Tennessee Valley Authority, $50,000,-
000; Boulder Canyon Dam, $38,000,000; supervising
architect, public buildings, $39,094,360; Coast Guard,
$24,833,535; flood control, the Mississippi and Mis-
souri rivers, $96,928,108; Quartermaster Corps of the
Army, for housing, $57,797,776; rivers and harbors,
$98,699,700; sea coast defenses, $20,250,000; Tri-
borough Bridge Authority, New York, $44,200,000;
Midtown Hudson Tunnel, New York, $37,500,000;
forest highways, $15,000,000; forest roads and trails,
$10,000,000; soil erosion control, $5,000,000; Grand
Coulee project, Columbia River Basin, $63,000,000;
Casper-Alcova project, Wyoming, $22,700,000; Pub-
lic Health Service, $39,094,360; construction naval
shore stations, $23,662,652; low-cost housing projects

in various cities, $37,239,958; Navy Department, for various department bureau activities, hospitals, etc., $30,118,024; and, for the aeronautical, lighthouse, geological survey and other Department of Commerce activities, $8,870,934." *

But these are *allocations,* not funds in current expenditure, and it is on account of this fact that complaints are being raised in many quarters. There are several difficulties that seem to have accounted for the exasperating delay in getting the program started. The very magnitude of the program is one of them. The early lack of preparation is another. During all the months that the Congress was legislating and when it was reasonably well-known that some such program would be enacted, little or no adequate preparation was made to receive it. Countless projects could have been tentatively prepared and approved pending authorization, so that as soon as the bill became a law the program could commence. Restrictions in the regulations and legal and other barriers in the States and smaller localities impeded the progress. There is also considerable hesitation in the States with respect to any activity likely to increase taxation, and this has made them reluctant to coöperate with the Federal Government. It may well be too, that the regulations on loans and funds so restricts the chances for large, pork-barrel, profits that there is little initiative upon the part of many citizens who in normal times would be found active. Much of the trouble is due also to sheer ignorance upon the part of public and other agencies of

* Item in the New York *Times,* October 23, 1933.

the machinery placed at their disposal by the Act. Here again, there is need for a sound, well-organized contact unit in strategic centers of States, the larger municipalities, and even in many smaller communities. The public works program actually needs to spend some of its money on a "public service corps" to acquaint the communities of the nation in a more positive way than they are now informed by newspapers, radios, and speeches, with the possibilities of coöperating in the public works program. Such State Advisory Committees as have been formed and limited field forces moving about the country constitute the loosest kind of contacts for a program as stupendous as the one outlined. Furthermore, the Federal organization itself should not relinquish its search for opportunities where it can put the program to work directly, because it ought to realize that a large number of groups about the country are not at all in sympathy with the principles, the directions, and the schemes of the Recovery Program, and will delay them by ways far more effective by reason of their subtlety.

The program has a vital connection with stimulating private enterprise. Its objects are to increase purchasing power from the bottom up, with high standards of compensation, while spreading work through shorter hours. Difficult as it has been to start the machinery, now that the allocations are made, the program should begin to penetrate down to the people and continue to do so with increasing momentum. If it fails to do this within another sixty days, Congress will doubtless commence an investigation to see where the fault lies.

The other category of public works is best illustrated by four projects: Subsistence Homesteads, the Public Works Emergency Housing Corporation, the Columbia River development projects, and the Muscle Shoals project.

The first, the formation of subsistence homesteads, is in the nature of an experiment. The sum of $25,000,-000 was set apart by the National Industrial Recovery Act "for aiding the redistribution of the overbalance of population in industrial centers . . . for making loans for and otherwise aiding in the purchase of subsistence homesteads." The fund created is a revolving fund and may possibly stretch far beyond its present service. The trial plan under this Act is as follows: a farm has been acquired in West Virginia comprising some 1,100 acres. The surrounding area contained coal mines which have been idle for years it is stated. Thousands of coal miners and their families are leading a precarious existence. It is proposed to settle 200 of such families on this land, giving to each some two to four acres of land and building upon it modest houses for their occupancy. Expenditures per family will be about $2,000 which it is to repay over a period of twenty-five years, the money going into the revolving funds for similar employment. A model community will be laid out with a school to serve as the social center. To aid the community at the outset, a government factory manufacturing twine for the Postoffice Department will be set up, while vocational training will prepare the people for handicrafts and other employments. By the combination of reasonably well-guaranteed employment and the opportunity to have subsistence gardens, it is hoped that the community will be able to make itself independent for a large part of its needs.

To every one sufficiently acquainted with some parts of the country where education is sadly lacking, where medical care is woefully inadequate, where numbers of people have remained far below the standards of living attained in other sections of the country, this plan will doubtless commend itself. And so long as this plan and others similar to it are confined to the basic principle of immediate rehabilitation few objections can be made. The present importance of the project is that it furnishes an outlet for distress once abundantly supplied by the frontier, an outlet which was definitely closed in the last decade of the 19th century. It thus meets a definite, but temporary, need. That it should become a national ideal beyond its present service of rehabilitation, is open to strong challenge.

The second project is in some sense similar to the above, except that rehabilitation is related to a state of things as well as to human beings. Capitalist economy has never looked upon slum clearance as a profit-making enterprise. If it went into the field at all it was merely to make an occasional venture in philanthropy. It might be demonstrated that capitalist economy was wrong in such an attitude, but that is not the point here. Whenever a project was desirable in the public interest and yet not capable of yielding an immediate profit to some entrepreneur, the Government finally had to undertake it. It has been so with many things that have become great public enterprises today. For years there has been an insistent cry for better, low-cost housing in cities. At the same time, there has been a reluctance to do anything drastic about ridding urban life of the unwholesomeness and social menace of slum districts. Slum clearance has at last entered that stage where the act of rehabilitation, if done at all, must be done by government.

Within the scope of the Public Works Administration, a Public Works Emergency Housing Corporation has been organized as a government undertaking. This public corporation will seek to meet two problems by clearing away slum areas and erecting on the sites modern low-cost apartment houses. The initial capital of the corporation will be about $200,000,000 and it is possible that it may borrow considerably larger, additional sums, since each project will be to some extent self-supporting. It will have at its command, it is stated, the powers of eminent domain for the acquisition of land which is necessary if extortions on the prices of sites are to be avoided. It will seek to enlist the aid of municipalities and semi-public agencies interested in the betterment of their communities. It will be immensely valuable to those cities capable of grasping the significance of the aid being offered to their people.

The third of these projects is somewhat different. It concerns the allocation of some $83,000,000 for a combined development on the Columbia River in the States of Oregon and Washington. Two power plants are to be built in the area, that of Grand Coulee on the Columbia River about seventy miles west of Spokane for which $63,000,000 has been allotted, and that at Bonneville, Oregon, about fifty miles east of Portland for which a first allotment of $20,000,000 has been made. Both projects contemplate the generation of electric power, while the latter will be part of a larger project for the improvement of navigation, flood control, and the provision of water for reclamation. Electric power is essentially a monopoly enterprise and until recent years its production, distribution and sale has been largely in the hands of private corporations.

Time and again throughout the country, the people have been inflamed by abuses and unfair practices in this field. One has only to read the volumes of testimony before the Federal Trade Commission to be amazed at the audacity, the deceit, and the misrepresentation which have characterized the operations of individuals and groups in the power industry. Public rate-making agencies were blocked in numerous efforts to control them. No amount of reforming zeal seemed to be capable of correcting the evils. Often an appeal to the courts accomplished nothing more than the creation of legal snarl which lasted for years while the people were compelled to submit to high rates for electric energy which had become a necessity. The private power companies and the bankers who drew from them in turn huge profits were for years blind to the extremes to which they were pushing their advantages. The Federal Trade Commission investigation revealed a multitude of evil practices and tactics in the private power industry, and its reports opened the eyes of Congress, State legislators, and thoughtful people all over the country. An "Insull" episode here and there dramatized the situation. Such events destroyed a considerable part of the pride with which many citizens had looked upon power development in private hands. The demand for public ownership, which had been increasing in volume for years and which had achieved some notable, if minor, results in various sections of the country, had to be met. It was met in such aids to public power development as the one above described.

It was also met by a fourth project, the creation of the Muscle Shoals power enterprise and the Tennessee River development plan. Ever since the war the Government had been unable to make any disposal of the magnificent plant at Muscle Shoals. Private power lobbies had blocked proposals for public operation. Their persistence, together with the clash of other conflicting interests, prevented the full use of one of the best power resources in the country. For more than ten years the deadlock continued, until at last an assertion of public rights prevailed.

Public Act No. 17 (H. R. 5081), approved by the President on May 18, 1933, was passed "To improve the navigability and to provide for the flood control of the Tennessee River; to provide for reforestation and proper use of marginal lands in the Tennessee Valley; to provide for the agricultural and industrial development of the said Valley; to provide for the national defense by the creation of a corporation for the operation of the Government properties at and near Muscle Shoals in the State of Alabama, and for other purposes." The Act creates a corporate body—the Tennessee Valley Authority—to which the President appoints a board of directors of three. Significantly, the law provides that "All members of the board shall be persons who profess a belief in the feasibility and wisdom of this Act." For too long public projects had been hampered, if not defeated, by subtle, unsympathetic direction.

The new corporation has practically all the powers and obligations of a private corporation and such implied powers as are "necessary or appropriate for the exercise of the powers herein specifically conferred upon the Corporation." This includes the right to acquire real estate by eminent domain and take title in the name of the United States. Some of the powers of the Corporation are as follows: To construct dams, reservoirs, power houses, tranmission lines, navigation projects, and incidental works on the Tennessee River and its tributaries. To contract with commercial producers, or itself manufacture and sell fertilizers and their ingredients and fixed nitrogen. To work in connection with national, state, district and county farms and experimental stations and with farmers. It will serve the national defense needs of the United States. It may produce, distribute, and sell electric power, either to private corporations or individuals, or to states, counties, and municipalities. It may lease properties and transmission lines. If it sells its power to private persons or corporations for redistribution and sale "for profit," it shall require such sales to be made "at prices that shall not exceed a schedule fixed by the board from time to time as reasonable, just and fair."

A wider development than the mere production of power is contemplated by the Act. The President is authorized to make surveys and plans for the use, conservation, and development of the Tennessee River Basin and for the general welfare of the citizens throughout the surrounding area. He is to recommend legislation to Congress, as well as to carry out the Act, "All for the general purpose of fostering an orderly and proper physical, economic, and social development of said areas." The Corporation has the authority to issue and sell serial bonds not exceeding $50,000,000 at 3½ per cent interest. It has access to the Patent Office and to all other government departments for information, expert advice, and assistance. The United States reserves the right to take full possession in the event of war. The net proceeds from the sale of power and products of the Corporation, after deducting costs of operation, maintenance, depreciation, and amortization, and a reserve for operating capital, are to be paid into the Treasury of the United States. The Comptroller General will audit the transactions of the Corporation; and an annual report must be filed by the Corporation with the President and the Congress.

The four projects above described—subsistence homesteads, slum clearance, and the two power enterprises—are something apart from the usual public works activities. The "New Deal" did not create them; it was only the channel through which they emerged. They were due to appear and would have come irrespective of the medium, the Recovery Program or any other. They are projects which could not have been blocked much longer. Continued efforts to do so would have revealed a failure to understand their meaning, and invited their attainment in some other, more undesirable, fashion. These projects, then, are not accidents. They are being thrown up by strong forces underlying the political and social development of the country—forces which have been germinating for years and which are now entering a stage tending toward a maturity. They imply a reconstruction of the old economic processes based upon individual initiative and competition—a reconstitution designed to compel those elements to flow into new channels and toward different objectives. They confirm the principle of coöperation and at the same time broaden enormously the sphere in which coöperation must function.

In a statement issued early in November, President Roosevelt laid emphasis on employment, as distinguished from the "dole," and urged the speeding up of public works to take care of four million idle people. He called upon governors and mayors to join in a concerted national effort in this direction.

CHAPTER VIII

PRINCIPLES OF THE RECOVERY PROGRAM

THERE are two broad aspects of any program, of any set of comprehensive plans: (1) the large goals to be achieved; and (2) the means to be employed to attain them. So far as is possible within the compass of small space, the latter has been described in the previous parts of this document. It remains to consider the ends toward which the Recovery Program seems to be directed.

ENDS AND MEANS ARE INSEPARABLE

The laws under which men act are of considerable importance, but of far greater significance is the *attitude* with which men approach the laws, and the *principles* they profess to hold in their administration of the laws. What attitudes and principles lie behind the Recovery Program? Neither the President, his advisors, nor Congress has written a bill of particulars on this point. No single, succinct, statement exists. This does not establish the fact that there are no principles behind the Recovery Program; it merely makes the task of discovering them more difficult.

It is necessary, therefore, to go to the speeches of the President, of those associated with him and under his direction. Each part and act of the Recovery Program must be reëxamined with the question uppermost: What is this thing seeking to accomplish? For such a reëxamination, the reader is directed back to the several parts of the Program, to the laws enacted by Congress, where the policies of the legislation and the purposes sought have been written into the Acts and have been made a part of the machinery set up to carry them into effect. Some of the material from the principal speeches will be presented below.

First as to Industry and Transportation. In his inaugural address the President spoke of the things necessary in the task of restoration. "It can be helped," he said, "by national planning for and supervision of all forms of transportation and of communications and other utilities which have a definitely public character." Upon the signing of the National Industrial Recovery Act, the President revealed his attitude toward industry and labor in much more detail. "The law I have just signed," he declared, "was passed to put people back to work—to let them buy more of the products of the farms and factories and start our business at a living rate again. . . . It seems to me to be equally plain that no business which depends for existence on paying less than living wages to its workers has any right to continue in this country . . . and by living wages I mean more than a bare subsistence level —I mean the wages of decent living." And "decent living, widely spread among our 125,000,000 people, eventually means the opening up to industry of the richest market which the world has known." He recognizes the advent of the mass production principle by stating that only through decent, higher living standards, can the excess industrial plant capacity be absorbed.

All employers of labor must act in unison; no one alone can accomplish the nation's recovery. There must be "one single mass action, to improve the case of the workers on a scale never attempted in any nation." To industry, the President stated, ". . . we are putting in place of old principles of unchecked competition some new government controls. . . . Their purpose is to free business. . . ."—observing that "industry . . . has long insisted that, given the right to act in unison, it could do much for the general good which has hitherto been unlawful. From today it has that right." He was referring to the relaxation of the antitrust laws, but he cautioned ". . . the antitrust laws still stand firmly against monopolies that restrain trade and price-fixing which allow inordinate profits or unfairly high prices." Those who play the game for the general good, the President stated, must be protected from those who may seek selfish gains from the unselfishness of others.

In order to prevent prices from rising faster than renewed purchasing power, the President made a plea for the postponement of full initial profits at least for the first critical months. That he will not hesitate to curb those "who might thwart this great common purpose by seeking selfish advantage," the President made clear in his appeal to the nation in July: "There are adequate penalties in the law, but I am now asking the coöperation that comes from opinion and from conscience." Some of the subsequent developments under the NRA codes appear to bear out the fact that the President may substantiate his words on this point.

That he seeks to achieve a balance in the economic life of the nation also emerges from this July speech. A lasting prosperity cannot be attained "in a nation half boom and half broke; . . . the best way is for every one to be reasonably prosperous." Summing up his principles and the results attained in industry, the President, in his radio address of October 22, 1933, declared: "The secret of the NRA is coöperation." There has been much coöperation and there have been complaints. "We know there are chiselers. At the bottom of every case of criticism and obstruction we have found some selfish interest, some private axe to grind." But the results are encouraging. "I am convinced that at least 4,000,000 have been given employment. . . . [The NRA] has abolished child labor. It has eliminated the sweatshop. It has ended 60 cents a week paid in some mills and 80 cents a week paid in some mines. . . ." It is probably inaccurate to say that *all* cases of criticism and complaint represent a selfish interest, but it is not difficult to concede that there have been enough of such instances to give substantial support to the President's statement.

What of the attitudes of the President's associates or administrators on the aims in industry? In a brief filed with the Senate Finance Committee investigating economic problems under S. Res. 315, Mr. Donald R.

Richberg, who is now General Counsel to the NRA, declared: "No man with sufficient intelligence to be worthy of any attention can deny that a planned control of the great essential industries is absolutely essential. . . . The state socialist would seek this planned control through direct governmental operation of industries; . . . the reactionary individualist would withdraw political prohibitions against monopoly and leave the primary planning and control to be carried on by the owners and privately selected managers of private property, subject only to some limited regulation by government. . . ." Rejecting both of these, Mr. Richberg declared: "There remains . . . the program of the reconstructed individualist. I seek to represent him, as a man still living in the tradition of American liberty . . . [who] knows that the production and distribution of the necessities and common comforts of life must be planned and regulated so that a certain minimum standard of living can be obtained by all."

Respecting the method of procedure, Mr. Richberg stated: "The permanent remedy . . . is to enact the laws necessary to reorganize our political-economic system, so that our industries must be operated for the primary purpose of employing as many workers as possible at the highest possible wages, while paying the lowest possible compensation for the use of money and property that will induce all necessary investment. . . . We have been viewing industry upside down throughout the era of capitalism. The only object of primitive industry was to furnish a livelihood to the worker.

That should be the primary object and obligation of all industries today." He then described a plan for "self-government in industry" in which there would be no room for gamblers, profiteers, money-mad megalomaniacs, or commercial "Napoleons," "who wreck communities and nations of the present day in their pursuit of anti-social aims and insane ambitions"; but where "there would be room for great public servants entitled to wealth and power suited to their demonstrated capacity to serve their country."

Later, speaking from his position of General Counsel to the NRA, Mr. Richberg declared: "The industries of the nation should serve primarily the needs of the workers of the nation. . . . We will never have a fair distribution of the rewards of industry . . . except when there is a democratic writing of the rules under which men compete for the prizes of life and a democratic control of the interpretation and enforcement of those rules." In another speech (at Labor Day celebration, Memphis, Tennessee) he said: "Coöperative mechanisms must be developed to meet these needs." In a still later speech (at the Babson Institute, September 8, 1933) he pointed out the fact that business was no longer managed by "owners" but by "managers" who think of themselves as "proprietors" and who have been cheating the stockholders of big industrial and commercial enterprises as well as the public. One can scarcely pick up a single issue of a newspaper over recent months—detailing the enormous salaries of industrial leaders, bankers, railroad presidents, and the like; showing the stock manipulations of "insiders" for the benefit of their friends and relatives; describing the ingenious legal devices employed by persons of reputed integrity to evade the tax provisions of the law—without finding ample confirmation of Mr. Richberg's observation. In the same address, he stated that "there must be a general recognition of the social value and industrial service which only labor organizations could perform"; and that the dominant purpose of the whole program "must be to maintain a balance between production and consumption—not by a reactionary curtailment of production, but by a progressive increase of consumption." On this point of production and consumption, almost all supporters of the Recovery Program intimate that the first step may be a temporary curtailment of production in the interests of stabilizing a disorganized system —with the ultimate design of instituting a planned, orderly system, under which increased consumption can move forward without generating unbalance again in the future.

General Hugh Johnson has been in the public eye so long and so prominently that it is almost superfluous to canvass the principles he holds and the objectives he seeks. They are rather well-known, and only a few excerpts need be given here. In a statement made at one of the early hearings on the Retail Merchants' Code (August 22, 1933) he said: "During the war the industries of the country did get together and, by making common concessions and applying the general rule of equity, accomplished a very great object. Our object now is not the same as the object then, but the lesson that was learned then was that it is possible, by coöperation, to attain a great national object."

Neither the President nor Mr. Johnson, however, could neglect the fact for one moment that two things made the war effort possible—a shortage of labor which released enormous productive capacities locked up in machines for years, and the further fact of an acceptance of an enormous indebtedness, public and private. Both have a direct bearing upon the present Recovery Program which must work toward still shorter hours, and must bring about increased productivity through some other device than the creation of indebtedness which, as we have seen, has operated historically to lay the country low with a regularity that should prove a lesson for the present. On this very point, General Johnson made a shrewd observation in a later address (before the Illinois State Federation of Labor, Chicago, September 4, 1933) when he described the westward migrations of the pioneers toward free land and fresh opportunity as a "safety valve" of the old capitalist system. "The point about all this Nineteenth Century history is this," he said, "that just so long as every man had always at his door the road that led to such an escape from destitution and dissatisfaction, the system justified itself."

Speaking before the American Federation of Labor Convention on October 10, 1933, General Johnson reiterated the President's conception of a partnership between the Government and Industry. "The basic principles of the NRA are sound and simple," he said. "On the one hand they permit and encourage each great industry to organize and act as one under direct governmental supervision. . . . On the other hand they permit and encourage the workers in each industry to organize and act as one. . . . In other words this act asks for coöperation between industry, labor, and government as one great team, to preserve the economic health of the nation. . . ." "The purpose is to regulate the quantity of what goes in the hopper to the power of the country to consume what comes out of the spout. The purpose is to balance consumption with our enormous potential productivity—not by reducing production, but by increasing the power to consume by a more even distribution of the fruits of every man's endeavor."

So much for industry and transportation. What of agriculture? Many of the principles toward which the agricultural section of the Recovery Program has been addressed have already been discussed. In his inaugural address, the President stated that "we must frankly recognize the overbalance of population in our industrial centers and, by engaging on a national scale in a redistribution, endeavor to provide a better use of the land for those best fitted for the land." In his appeal to the nation he stated that "the two great barriers to a normal prosperity have been low farm prices and the creeping paralysis of unemployment." The Farm Act, he observed, "is based on the fact that the purchasing power of nearly half our population depends on adequate prices for farm products. We have been producing more of some crops than we consume or can sell in a depressed world market. The cure is not to produce so much." In his radio speech of October 22, he declared that he was not yet satisfied with the level of farm prices and that he was determined to continue to experiment until he raised them. The ultimate purpose, in the words of Mr. Henry A. Wallace, Secretary of Agriculture, is that "of adjusting our agriculture to the market that actually exists" and to correct the "wide disparity between the prices of the things the farmer sells and the things he buys." This, he says, is "a genuine disposition to work toward a balance between our major producing groups." Mr. George N. Peek, Administrator of the Agricultural Adjustment Act, confirms this in the observation that "the farm and industrial recovery programs are complementary, and each will profit greatly from success of the other."

In the field of finance, the President fired the opening gun in his inaugural address when he spoke of the money changers who "have fled from their high seats in the temple of our civilization." Admitting the necessity of a sally into rhetorical expression at the height of the money crisis and in the glamorous setting of an inauguration ceremony, what did the President really intend to do about finance in restoring the temple to the ancient truths? "The measure of restoration lies in the extent to which we apply social values more noble than mere monetary profit." The Recovery Program seeks to substantiate this by providing a stronger banking system, deposit insurance, the regulation of securities transactions by measures designed to insure legal honesty as well as fair dealings, with limited, reasonable profits. Through the gold policy it is evident that the President seeks to insulate the American economic system from what he termed "the accidents of international trade." His domestic objective is to "establish and maintain continuous control" of the monetary system in the interests of stabilized monetary units and the operation of a "managed currency."

Mr. Richberg was even more indignant over the tactics of the "money changers" than was the President. In the brief before the Senate Committee to which reference has been made, he stated: "You have listened to financiers who demand that a system of corporate organization and control be continued under which power and responsibility are so divorced that investors, workers, and consumers can be systematically betrayed and robbed by 'trustees' with little risk that any big thief will be sent to jail. . . . Although the conspicuous money-makers [embracing a larger group of men than the bankers alone] who presume to advise you have proved their ability to make themselves wealthy, it is far more important for this committee to realize that they have also proved their ability to make millions of people very poor. When they are credited with paying large dividends occasionally, they should be debited with paying low wages regularly. If they are to be applauded for producing brief eras of spotty prosperity, they should be denounced for producing long periods of general depression. . . . The profits that are frozen in marble and bronze were squeezed out of human beings who labored and suffered and made sacrifices of health and comfort and happiness in order that wealth might be accumulated in a few hands."

In his plan for the rehabilitation of the nation, Mr. Richberg would pay "the lowest possible compensation for the use of money and property that will induce all necessary investment." In all of the corporations set up by the Government, prices (when they are involved as in the Muscle Shoals project) must be fair, just, and reasonable, dividends must be limited to a fair, fixed return, and salaries paid must not be exorbitant.

In tendering loans and other financial aid to private industry, finance and commerce, the reduction of large salaries has been demanded. Mr. Joseph B. Eastman's move in that direction in the matter of salaries paid to railroad presidents is conspicuous. But more than that, the Federal Trade Commission has instituted an inquiry into executive-salary conditions of more than 2,000 corporations engaged in interstate commerce, whose stock is listed on the New York Stock or Curb Exchanges and whose capital assets exceed $1,000,000.

It may be assumed that this inquiry will be stopped by those whose interests are affected, if it is humanly possible to do it, and that there will be the usual complaints about government encroachment on private affairs. Indeed, it should be mentioned that, according to press reports, many attempts have been made to end the Senate inquiry into stock market practices and the corrupting methods associated with them. But that inquiry, under the direction of the committee's council, Mr. Ferdinand Pecora, still goes on vigorously under the Recovery Program.

What social principles govern relief in the Recovery Program? It has already been stated that the President has asserted that "nobody is going to starve in this country," and that provisions have been made to carry his declaration into effect. To the assurance of subsistence, he added that of security in his address on October 22: "If there is any family in the United States about to lose its home or about to lose its chattels, that family should telegraph at once either to the Farm Credit Administration or the Home-Owners Loan Corporation in Washington requesting their help."

Now we may turn to the political philosophy behind the Recovery Program. On the question of Government and the Constitution, the President has observed: "Our Constitution is so simple and practical that it is possible always to meet extraordinary needs by changes in emphasis and arrangement without loss of essential form." Speaking before the American Bar Association at Grand Rapids, Michigan, August 31, 1933, Attorney General Cummings stated: "There has not been the slightest fundamental departure from the form or nature of our government or the established order. . . . Every new power entrusted to the President has been conferred by the people, acting through their duly elected representatives. . . . The Congress has neither abdicated nor shirked its rights or its duties. . . . What is really happening is not an alteration in the established form or texture of government, but a change in the spirit and application of government. . . . The Constitution is no mere lawyer's document, but the whole of the Nation's life." The country awaits the answer of the Supreme Court.

On matters of economic philosophy, President Roosevelt has expressed his views in various forms. In his book *Looking Forward,* he spoke of many things all tending toward the same end—a common effort for the common good. "Business must think less of its own profit and more of the national function it performs." He spoke of "our mutual dependence one upon the other," of balanced economic units for "a common participation in the work of remedial measures, planned on the basis of a shared common life, the low as well as the high. . . . I plead not for a class control but for a true concert of interests." In his appeal to the nation he spoke of "everybody doing things together . . . people acting in a group . . . this great common effort." In his address on September 8, 1933, on the nation's welfare needs, he said: "All this community chest work, all of this uniting in the cause of meeting human needs, is based on that old word, 'Coöperation.' " In his address at the unveiling of the Samuel Gompers Memorial at Washington, October 8, 1933, the President said: "There are some who think in terms of dollars and cents instead of terms of human lives." Returning again to his theme of the "money changers," the President in his radio broadcast to the nation on October 22, 1933, rendered account of his stewardship in this question: "How are we constructing the edifice of recovery—the temple which, when completed, will no longer be a temple of money-changers or of beggars, but rather a temple dedicated to and maintained, for a greater social justice, a greater welfare for America—the habitation of a sound economic life?"

Seeking through Mr. Richberg's speeches for the philosophy of the Recovery Program, we find that "The fact that a man is 'restrained' by law does not mean that he is thereby deprived of freedom. The only way that men can be set free is by imposing restraints on the abuse of freedom." Speaking of the broader purposes, he said: "We are seeking to create self-interest in coöperation." In his Labor Day address he referred to "the direct action of the Government of the United States in behalf of all the people." Later in the same address he declared: "There is nothing destructive or antagonistic to the institution of private property in the demand that human beings must be kept alive, protected from want, and maintained in good health before properties can be made income producing." In his Babson Institute address, he said: "It is not right that any man should sabotage this coöperative movement of which he is a part, or sabotage the administration of this law, which was enacted and is being administered for the advancement of the general welfare." Speaking of the people "working at incredible and exhausting speed in Washington," he declared that "practically all these people are attempting a truly coöperative spirit to prove that the American people are capable of an achievement without precedent; the reorganization of a political-economic system without a revolution of violence," a task which can be accomplished "because there is no change at-

tempted in the final objectives of the American people
. . . the goal of the greatest possible freedom and
security for every American citizen."

Other officials of the administration, such as
Frances Perkins, Secretary of Labor, speak of "economic coöperative effort," or "mass effort," of "fair
competition," of the "tremendous collective organizations we have built up," of "economic balance," of a
"movement for the benefit of the whole people," of
"competition in excellent buying, in prudent buying,
good merchandising" as against "ruthless price competition and price cutting," of the effort "to conquer
disparities," a "national movement toward a common
end," a movement "for the whole American people."
General Johnson, always colorful, always dynamic,
always impulsive, spoke of Alexander Hamilton who
"proposed a system under which their [the people's]
affairs would be taken care of by the good and the wise
and the great. . . . The trouble with that has been that
the good and the wise and the great have fallen down
on the job and that education and training has so
evened things up that nobody has a monopoly on
goodness and greatness and wisdom any more."

Writing in the New York *Times* Sunday magazine
(October 29, 1933) on "The Social Economics of the
New Deal," Professor A. A. Berle, Jr. is more realistic.
He recognizes that the "old economic forces still work
and they do produce a balance after a while. But they
take so long to do it and they crush so many men in
the process that the strain on the social system becomes
intolerable." Addressing himself to the question, "Will

this gigantic attempt to mold an individualist, capitalist system into a directed economic effort produce the result?", he referred to the freedom of mind with which those who planned the Recovery Program had acted. He said: "Those of us who had the privilege of working on the original plan began with the assumption that what we needed most was a machine that worked. Whether it was rugged individualism, Fascism, Communism, Socialism, or what-not, made not the slightest bit of difference." Then he discussed the alternative to the Recovery Program whereby "the Government of the United States, forgetting all about the Constitution," would "commandeer everything and everyone," turning the property into government property, the factories into government production agencies, directing what and how much is to be produced, giving to each citizen a red card entitling him to a share of the total goods produced, and which under proper guidance and control, might possibly give to each citizen in terms of goods and services "an income . . . equivalent to what $5,000 a year income will buy now." He could imagine an American Government doing that if it had to—"but only if it had to," because there are enormous implications involved in any such an apparently simple procedure. It is on account of this alternative that the Roosevelt administration must succeed in its experiment, he holds. Then he closed with what may well be termed the entire keynote of the Recovery Program: "In a world in which revolutions just now are coming easily, the New Deal chose the more difficult course of moderation and rebuilding."

Of necessity attention has been confined here to the domestic aspects of the Recovery Program, but phases of foreign trade and relations are also involved. Here, too, the President has set forth fundamental principles. After the panic which opened in 1893, the party of the new imperialism, speaking through such leaders as Albert J. Beveridge, referred to the crisis in domestic economy—to the surpluses of goods that could not be sold at a profit at home, and declared that it would find these outlets abroad by the methods long employed by Great Britain. President Franklin D. Roosevelt has, by implication at least, repudiated that possibility as an escape from the domestic jam and has shifted the emphasis. America is to find relief from the crisis, not by outward thrusts of national power conquering markets, but by an intensive and coöperative cultivation of the national garden. In his inaugural address he said: "Through this program of action we address ourselves to putting our own national house in order. . . . Our international trade relations, though vastly important, are in point of time and necessity secondary to the establishment of a sound national economy. . . . I shall spare no effort to restore world trade by international economic readjustment, but the emergency at home cannot wait on that accomplishment. . . . The basic thought that guides these specific means of national recovery is not narrowly nationalistic. It is the insistence, as a first consideration, upon the interdependence of the various elements in and parts of the United States of America. . . . In the field of world policy I would dedicate this nation to the policy of the good neighbor—the neighbor who resolutely respects himself and, because he does so, respects the rights of others. . . ."

From this review of the Recovery Program, it is necessary or possible to record *new* things that mark or seem to mark a departure from the past—the opening of another period in American history; and, if so, what is their nature?

1. The Recovery Program accepts the inexorable development of combination in industry, abandons all faith in the healing power of dissolution and prosecution; and makes use of combination in planning, fixing responsibility, and seeking to hold down monopoly profiteering.

2. The Recovery Program recognizes the right of labor to organize, to be represented in industry, and to participate in the administration of the Program.

3. The Recovery Program calls upon millions of individuals in industry and agriculture, who have hitherto been pursuing their own interests at pleasure, to coöperate in adjusting production, setting prices, and maintaining standards—thus making imperative a new economic education on a colossal scale.

4. The Recovery Program attacks the historic method of distributing wealth through the system of price and wage competition, and substitutes, in part at least, price and wage fixing, haltingly and tentatively, no doubt, but still positively.

5. In attacking the historic price system, the administrators of the Recovery Program are coming to

recognize the fact that advance in this direction involves throwing daylight throughout the entire structure of industry and agriculture, illuminating the dark recesses where secrecy and manipulation accompany the struggle over the distribution of wealth, which arises from the conflict between private property and social needs.

6. In giving to agriculture an equality in principle with industry, the Recovery Program recognizes its present inequality in the battle with highly organized capitalism over prices and profits—its inequality in organization, in wealth, in educational equipment, and leadership, and its incapacity to defend itself against the cramping and draining effect of highly organized machine industries. For years students of economy have been pointing out that "agriculture is doomed" in this deadly competition. Erich Zimmerman, in his excellent work on World Resources, has revealed with startling precision the hand-writing on the wall. Now the Government of the United States attacks the problem thus presented.

7. Implicit in all this is a call, in the Recovery Program, for a changed conception of economy and life. For more than a hundred years American economy has been essentially speculative and a dominant national ideal has been that of getting rich as quickly as possible. Even agriculture has been a huge venture in land speculation rather than a way of life. The Stock Market has been a kind of national shrine. It has been not the few but the many that have taken part in this grand gamble. At this hour there is no way of knowing

in advance the outcome of a national plebiscite on the following proposition: Would you rather have a gambler's chance of becoming a millionaire or a guarantee of a reasonable security and modest way of life? In insisting upon stabilization, steady price levels, competition in service only, and reasonable security for all, the Recovery Program runs contrary to a powerful American tradition and demands for its realization a reversal of attitude in the minds of the millions who have had as their ideal the lucky wheat or stock speculator, with his town and country houses, his yachts and jewels, and his place in the affections of the great newspapers. In other words, the Recovery Program places a strain on human nature as long revealed in American conceptions of economy.

8. The Recovery Program repudiates the idea that the misery of the unemployed poor is due to their improvidence and provides government assurance of maintenance, at least, and government assistance in developing employment opportunities.

9. Through its banking, credit, public-corporation, process-taxing, and railroad measures, the Recovery Program is moving in the direction of a new economic sequence which subjects private interests to a broad nationalization.

10. The Recovery Program surrenders the official thesis, long held, that foreign trade is the only outlet for "surpluses," that such an outlet is possible, and that it must be secured by using all engines of state in the field of foreign relations. For this thesis it substitutes the proposition that domestic economy must be

made to function in a manner to keep industry at a high tempo and effect an efficient distribution of the fruits of industry in the home market. Followed to its logical conclusion, this conception will lead to revolutionary adjustments in foreign trade and foreign relations.

If in these things clear-cut novelty is not discernible, there is in them a sharpness and weight of emphasis sufficient to make the New Deal signalize a break with the historic past and the coming of a future collectivist in character.

EPILOGUE

What has been the reception accorded to the Recovery Program by the country? It seems well within the range of truth to say that never in the history of the United States has anything like such a drastic program of legislation and administrative orders been accepted with as little bitter and dogmatic opposition. Conservative business interests which, in ordinary times, would have resisted such state intervention to the last ditch, have coöperated with the President in a manner scarcely to have been expected by those familiar with the hostility displayed toward Bryanism, Progressivism, and the New Freedom of President Wilson. The widespread paralysis of national economy and the apparent inability of those interests to cope with the crisis by their own action between 1929 and 1933 disconcerted them, spread distrust among them, and deprived them of their old unshakeable assurance. They had no alternative program, except to do nothing, to accept ruinous liquidation, to let "nature take its course"; but they were not certain that that policy of *laissez faire* would not end in a bigger disaster. The faith of capitalists in themselves, in their ability to conduct national and international industry, in their historic rôle had been shaken. They had no rallying point, save the President with a program.

Of detailed and sporadic criticism there was bound to be an abundance. The new legislation and the codes, launching economy on new experiments, were full of uncertainties, necessarily. There was no way of telling in advance just what was to be done down to the last item. Constant improvisation was inescapable. Leaders in numerous and complicated branches of industry were suddenly called upon, like the Fathers of the Republic in 1787, to make constitutions of government for themselves. The task called for statesmanlike qualities of the highest order, and those qualities were hard to find in the ranks of industry. There were many great directors and managers in industries, men who knew their respective areas of operations and were competent in them; but there were few who had thought about their branches of industry or industry itself as a whole. To put the case in the language of one among them: "I knew my company's business from A to Z, but I had never given any thought to the business in which the company was engaged, as one concern among many." In this situation many businessmen were exasperated with the confusion and uncertainty which accompanied the introduction of the NRA program and with good enough reason; but exasperation was not necessarily opposition in principle— opposition based on contrary hopes and principles.

The frankest criticism emerged from other quarters. Communists, of course, assailed it as a form of capitalist dictatorship and appealed to the usual formula—

the substitution of a proletarian dictatorship. Socialists were divided; some saw in the New Deal a step in the direction of general nationalization; others saw Fascism as an outcome. Conservative elements in the President's own party, timidly at first and later more openly, began to recite portions of the well-known creed of *laissez faire*. Although most leaders of Republican persuasion loyally coöperated with President Roosevelt, many Republican politicians, naturally looking to the repair of their fences, commenced to wonder how some kind of opposition could be organized, to get the offices, if for no other purposes. They soon had their formulas for the occasion: the country was well on the road to recovery any way and the Roosevelt program was retarding it; the Constitution was in danger; NRA was headed for socialism; the individualistic enterprise which had made America great was being stifled by the new bureaucracy. By the late autumn of 1933 it became evident that a strong opposition, composed of many discordant elements, was taking form and gaining in momentum.

What are its prospects? Students of history have witnessed powerful governments, apparently entrenched for the ages, overturned with the speed of a storm. They have witnessed the passions of men, bitterly divided in interest and outlook, temporarily united in undermining and destroying a common foe. Such things are among the possibilities and probabilities of history. On that score there can be no doubt. But students of history know also that on the morning after every overturn the action of policy must take the place

of the action of negation, that in the divided ranks of
the victors some direction of policy and measure must
come. Since this is true, those who look beyond securing for themselves a floating timber amid the wreck
will be moved to inquire: By what processes will the
Roosevelt Administration consolidate its forces for
the defense of its position? If it is ousted, what next?

As Mr. Roosevelt recognized in his campaign, referring pertinently enough to the writings of James Madi-
son, politics is concerned with the eternal conflict of
interests in society. To what interests will he appeal in
consolidating his forces for defense? It is not likely
that he can or will seek to marshal the forces of great
industry and banking, after the fashion of Marcus A.
Hanna and William McKinley. His chief opposition is
likely to come from that source. That being so, he
will be compelled, it seems, to appeal to the great body
of the lower middle class, laborers, and farmers, to
attempt to consolidate them in support of a program
even more drastic than that contemplated by the legislation of 1933. That task will not be easy; nor will it
be easy to reconcile the conflicting ideas and interests
of the middle class, labor, and agriculture in case of
victory; but the strong statesman attacks the impossible before he surrenders.

What next, in case the President and his program
are repudiated? A fortunate, though short-lived "up-
turn in business" might save the victors from the pain
of thought, should they be led by politicians rather
than statesmen. But it is likely that the scars of the
depression will not disappear soon, and that the victors

would have to frame a program of their own. Will it be the program of 1928, 1908, or 1897? That will be impossible, for history does not repeat itself. Will all the great pieces of recovery legislation be repealed? That seldom happens in a political overturn. Will the trade combinations and associations established under the codes be subjected again to prosecution under the antitrust laws or allowed to continue as uncontrolled monopolies? Does anyone familiar with the concentration movement of the past fifty years believe that a dissolution of combinations into competing units can really be effected? If uncontrolled monopolies be authorized to pursue their own course, can they keep industry running at a high tempo, avoid devastating crises, provide adequate employment, and satisfy the demand of farmers for equalizing prices? Evidently the prospect before the party of opposition on the day of its triumph over the New Deal will not be simple or pleasing.

In the matter of larger judgment, the verdict of contemporary thought in historiography is plain. That thought has arrived at the fundamental conclusion that history, of which the New Deal is a phase in brief time, is a movement of ideas and interests ever evolving together, reciprocally affecting each other, with interests now advancing far ahead of ideas and ideas now advancing far ahead of interests, ever producing tensions in society—tensions which must be adjusted either by reason or force. The great economic interests of the United States have been advancing with electric speed under the impacts of technology and organization, while the ruling ideas, appropriate to the age of the tallow candle and ox cart, have lagged behind, creating a great tension of which the present crisis is a special manifestation. This movement of ideas and interests will continue, for of such is the nature of history, which will not stop for President Roosevelt or Andrew D. Mellon. It will continue unless and until an appropriate adjustment is made or until it breaks apart society itself. It is in the light of world history, not as a battle of political kites and crows, that the New Deal must be viewed and judged. By the history now in the making and to be made, it and all other earthly designs will be judged, whatever we do or say. Beyond that great tribunal there lies no appeal.

It is from the standpoint of contemporary historical thought that criticism of, as well as sympathy for, the Recovery Program may be most cogently expressed. If that Program is regarded as a finality, then history cannot accept it, for history knows no finality except death—the bodily career of Julius Cæsar has finally closed. If the Program is considered as a new economic mechanism guaranteed to produce continuing prosperity and social security, history must reject it as capitalism has been rejected, for the reason that economy is only one phase of the cultural life which sustains civilization. If the Program is really treated by its sponsors as a program rather than a broad and flexible frame of reference for directing immediate thought and action, history may now record its failure and the coming eclipse of those who unreservedly commit themselves to it. At best the Program can only be regarded as the beginning of a transition.

INDEX

Aeronautical lighthouse, geological survey, and other activities, appropriation for, 133.

Agricultural Adjustment Act, 49, 89; indicates some of the purposes for which President's powers have been granted, 112; how they may be utilized, 112.

Agricultural commodities, basic, provisions of Farm Relief Act concerning, 78-80.

Agricultural Marketing Act, 89.

Agriculture, Dept. of, report concerning decline in farm values, 8.

Airplanes, increase in use of, 63.

Allen, Frederick L., in *Only Yesterday*, 4.

Annalist, report of sales of Stock Exchange for Oct. 1929, 4.

Arbitration, National Board of, its personnel, 52; its functions, 53.

Bank deposits, up to close of fiscal year in June, 1931, 13; temporary insurance of, 107; permanent insurance plans, 107.

Bank holiday, 18.

"Banking Act of 1933," provisions of, 99, 100.

Banking Emergency, Documents and Statements Pertaining to the, U. S. Treasury Publications, 17.

Banks, status of, June, 1932, 12, 13; reopening of, 24; not permitted to reopen, 26; steps to free deposits in closed, 27.

Barter, as an effort to provide relief, 11.

Beer bill, 31.

Berle, Prof. A. A., Jr., in *Times*, on "The Social Economics of the New Deal," 158, 159.

Beveridge, Albert J., referring to 1893 crisis, 160.

"Blanket Code," 53, 57.

"Blue Eagle," 60.

Blue Eagle Division of NRA, Washington headquarters of, 53; its field staff, 53; principal object of, 54.

Bonneville, Oregon, power plant at, 138.

"Bonus Army," of Hoover's administration, 123.

Boulder Canyon Dam, appropriation for, 132.

Budget, the government, 28; efforts to balance, 29-31; Roosevelt dual system, 31-34.

Capital stock tax, 31.

"Carriers' Act," 73.

Cash, rush for, 18.

Casper-Alcova project, appropriation for, 132.

Chase, Stuart, on barter, 10.

"Child Labor," 53, 58; elimination of, under NRA, 146.

"Chiseler," the, 59; an example of, 79, 146.

Citizens' Civilian Conservation Corps, their activities, 123.

Clearing-house certificates, 18, 19.

Coast Guard, appropriation for, 132.

Codes, formulation of, under